# Monthly Profit Tracker

| Month | Total Spend | Total Sales | Total Profit |
|---|---|---|---|
|  |  |  |  |
|  |  |  |  |
|  |  |  |  |
|  |  |  |  |
|  |  |  |  |
|  |  |  |  |
|  |  |  |  |
|  |  |  |  |
|  |  |  |  |
|  |  |  |  |
|  |  |  |  |
|  |  |  |  |
|  |  |  |  |
|  |  |  |  |
|  |  |  |  |
|  |  |  |  |
|  |  |  |  |
|  |  |  |  |
|  |  |  |  |
|  |  |  |  |
|  |  |  |  |
|  |  |  |  |
|  |  |  |  |
|  |  |  |  |
|  |  |  |  |
|  |  |  |  |
|  |  |  |  |
|  |  |  |  |

# Purchase & Sales Tracker

DATES FROM _____

| Item | Purchase Date | Sale Date | Sale Website | Purchase Price | Sale Price | Profit |
|------|---------------|-----------|--------------|----------------|------------|--------|
|  |  |  |  |  |  |  |
|  |  |  |  |  |  |  |
|  |  |  |  |  |  |  |
|  |  |  |  |  |  |  |
|  |  |  |  |  |  |  |
|  |  |  |  |  |  |  |
|  |  |  |  |  |  |  |
|  |  |  |  |  |  |  |
|  |  |  |  |  |  |  |
|  |  |  |  |  |  |  |
|  |  |  |  |  |  |  |
|  |  |  |  |  |  |  |
|  |  |  |  |  |  |  |
|  |  |  |  |  |  |  |
|  |  |  |  |  |  |  |
|  |  |  |  |  |  |  |
|  |  |  |  |  |  |  |
|  |  |  |  |  |  |  |
|  |  |  |  |  |  |  |
|  |  |  |  |  |  |  |
|  |  |  |  |  |  |  |
|  |  |  |  |  |  |  |
|  |  |  |  |  |  |  |
|  |  |  |  |  |  |  |
|  |  |  |  |  |  |  |
|  |  |  |  |  |  |  |
|  |  |  |  |  |  |  |

Total

# Purchase & Sales Tracker

DATES FROM _____

| Item | Purchase Date | Sale Date | Sale Website | Purchase Price | Sale Price | Profit |
|---|---|---|---|---|---|---|
|  |  |  |  |  |  |  |
|  |  |  |  |  |  |  |
|  |  |  |  |  |  |  |
|  |  |  |  |  |  |  |
|  |  |  |  |  |  |  |
|  |  |  |  |  |  |  |
|  |  |  |  |  |  |  |
|  |  |  |  |  |  |  |
|  |  |  |  |  |  |  |
|  |  |  |  |  |  |  |
|  |  |  |  |  |  |  |
|  |  |  |  |  |  |  |
|  |  |  |  |  |  |  |
|  |  |  |  |  |  |  |
|  |  |  |  |  |  |  |
|  |  |  |  |  |  |  |
|  |  |  |  |  |  |  |
|  |  |  |  |  |  |  |
|  |  |  |  |  |  |  |
|  |  |  |  |  |  |  |
|  |  |  |  |  |  |  |
|  |  |  |  |  |  |  |
|  |  |  |  |  |  |  |
|  |  |  |  |  |  |  |
|  |  |  |  |  |  |  |
|  |  |  |  |  |  |  |
|  |  |  |  |  |  |  |
|  |  |  |  |  |  |  |
|  |  |  |  |  |  |  |
|  |  |  |  |  |  |  |

Total

# Purchase & Sales Tracker

DATES FROM _____

| Item | Purchase Date | Sale Date | Sale Website | Purchase Price | Sale Price | Profit |
|---|---|---|---|---|---|---|
| | | | | | | |
| | | | | | | |
| | | | | | | |
| | | | | | | |
| | | | | | | |
| | | | | | | |
| | | | | | | |
| | | | | | | |
| | | | | | | |
| | | | | | | |
| | | | | | | |
| | | | | | | |
| | | | | | | |
| | | | | | | |
| | | | | | | |
| | | | | | | |
| | | | | | | |
| | | | | | | |
| | | | | | | |
| | | | | | | |
| | | | | | | |
| | | | | | | |
| | | | | | | |
| | | | | | | |
| | | | | | | |
| | | | | | | |
| | | | | | | |

Total | | |

# Purchase & Sales Tracker

DATES FROM _____

| Item | Purchase Date | Sale Date | Sale Website | Purchase Price | Sale Price | Profit |
|------|---------------|-----------|--------------|----------------|------------|--------|
|      |               |           |              |                |            |        |
|      |               |           |              |                |            |        |
|      |               |           |              |                |            |        |
|      |               |           |              |                |            |        |
|      |               |           |              |                |            |        |
|      |               |           |              |                |            |        |
|      |               |           |              |                |            |        |
|      |               |           |              |                |            |        |
|      |               |           |              |                |            |        |
|      |               |           |              |                |            |        |
|      |               |           |              |                |            |        |
|      |               |           |              |                |            |        |
|      |               |           |              |                |            |        |
|      |               |           |              |                |            |        |
|      |               |           |              |                |            |        |
|      |               |           |              |                |            |        |
|      |               |           |              |                |            |        |
|      |               |           |              |                |            |        |
|      |               |           |              |                |            |        |
|      |               |           |              |                |            |        |
|      |               |           |              |                |            |        |
|      |               |           |              |                |            |        |
|      |               |           |              |                |            |        |
|      |               |           |              |                |            |        |
|      |               |           |              |                |            |        |
|      |               |           |              |                |            |        |
|      |               |           |              |                |            |        |
|      |               |           |              |                |            |        |

Total

# Purchase & Sales Tracker

DATES FROM _____

| Item | Purchase Date | Sale Date | Sale Website | Purchase Price | Sale Price | Profit |
|---|---|---|---|---|---|---|
|  |  |  |  |  |  |  |
|  |  |  |  |  |  |  |
|  |  |  |  |  |  |  |
|  |  |  |  |  |  |  |
|  |  |  |  |  |  |  |
|  |  |  |  |  |  |  |
|  |  |  |  |  |  |  |
|  |  |  |  |  |  |  |
|  |  |  |  |  |  |  |
|  |  |  |  |  |  |  |
|  |  |  |  |  |  |  |
|  |  |  |  |  |  |  |
|  |  |  |  |  |  |  |
|  |  |  |  |  |  |  |
|  |  |  |  |  |  |  |
|  |  |  |  |  |  |  |
|  |  |  |  |  |  |  |
|  |  |  |  |  |  |  |
|  |  |  |  |  |  |  |
|  |  |  |  |  |  |  |
|  |  |  |  |  |  |  |
|  |  |  |  |  |  |  |
|  |  |  |  |  |  |  |
|  |  |  |  |  |  |  |
|  |  |  |  |  |  |  |

**Total**

# Purchase & Sales Tracker

DATES FROM _____

| Item | Purchase Date | Sale Date | Sale Website | Purchase Price | Sale Price | Profit |
|---|---|---|---|---|---|---|
|  |  |  |  |  |  |  |
|  |  |  |  |  |  |  |
|  |  |  |  |  |  |  |
|  |  |  |  |  |  |  |
|  |  |  |  |  |  |  |
|  |  |  |  |  |  |  |
|  |  |  |  |  |  |  |
|  |  |  |  |  |  |  |
|  |  |  |  |  |  |  |
|  |  |  |  |  |  |  |
|  |  |  |  |  |  |  |
|  |  |  |  |  |  |  |
|  |  |  |  |  |  |  |
|  |  |  |  |  |  |  |
|  |  |  |  |  |  |  |
|  |  |  |  |  |  |  |
|  |  |  |  |  |  |  |
|  |  |  |  |  |  |  |
|  |  |  |  |  |  |  |
|  |  |  |  |  |  |  |
|  |  |  |  |  |  |  |
|  |  |  |  |  |  |  |
|  |  |  |  |  |  |  |
|  |  |  |  |  |  |  |
|  |  |  |  |  |  |  |
|  |  |  |  |  |  |  |
|  |  |  |  |  |  |  |
|  |  |  |  |  |  |  |

Total

# Purchase & Sales Tracker

DATES FROM _____

| Item | Purchase Date | Sale Date | Sale Website | Purchase Price | Sale Price | Profit |
|---|---|---|---|---|---|---|
| | | | | | | |
| | | | | | | |
| | | | | | | |
| | | | | | | |
| | | | | | | |
| | | | | | | |
| | | | | | | |
| | | | | | | |
| | | | | | | |
| | | | | | | |
| | | | | | | |
| | | | | | | |
| | | | | | | |
| | | | | | | |
| | | | | | | |
| | | | | | | |
| | | | | | | |
| | | | | | | |
| | | | | | | |
| | | | | | | |
| | | | | | | |
| | | | | | | |
| | | | | | | |
| | | | | | | |
| | | | | | | |
| | | | | | | |
| | | | | | | |
| | | | | | | |

Total

# Purchase & Sales Tracker

DATES FROM _____

| Item | Purchase Date | Sale Date | Sale Website | Purchase Price | Sale Price | Profit |
|------|---------------|-----------|--------------|----------------|------------|--------|
|      |               |           |              |                |            |        |
|      |               |           |              |                |            |        |
|      |               |           |              |                |            |        |
|      |               |           |              |                |            |        |
|      |               |           |              |                |            |        |
|      |               |           |              |                |            |        |
|      |               |           |              |                |            |        |
|      |               |           |              |                |            |        |
|      |               |           |              |                |            |        |
|      |               |           |              |                |            |        |
|      |               |           |              |                |            |        |
|      |               |           |              |                |            |        |
|      |               |           |              |                |            |        |
|      |               |           |              |                |            |        |
|      |               |           |              |                |            |        |
|      |               |           |              |                |            |        |
|      |               |           |              |                |            |        |
|      |               |           |              |                |            |        |
|      |               |           |              |                |            |        |
|      |               |           |              |                |            |        |
|      |               |           |              |                |            |        |
|      |               |           |              |                |            |        |
|      |               |           |              |                |            |        |
|      |               |           |              |                |            |        |
|      |               |           |              |                |            |        |
|      |               |           |              |                |            |        |
|      |               |           |              |                |            |        |

Total

# Purchase & Sales Tracker

DATES FROM _____

| Item | Purchase Date | Sale Date | Sale Website | Purchase Price | Sale Price | Profit |
|------|---------------|-----------|--------------|----------------|------------|--------|
|  |  |  |  |  |  |  |
|  |  |  |  |  |  |  |
|  |  |  |  |  |  |  |
|  |  |  |  |  |  |  |
|  |  |  |  |  |  |  |
|  |  |  |  |  |  |  |
|  |  |  |  |  |  |  |
|  |  |  |  |  |  |  |
|  |  |  |  |  |  |  |
|  |  |  |  |  |  |  |
|  |  |  |  |  |  |  |
|  |  |  |  |  |  |  |
|  |  |  |  |  |  |  |
|  |  |  |  |  |  |  |
|  |  |  |  |  |  |  |
|  |  |  |  |  |  |  |
|  |  |  |  |  |  |  |
|  |  |  |  |  |  |  |
|  |  |  |  |  |  |  |
|  |  |  |  |  |  |  |
|  |  |  |  |  |  |  |
|  |  |  |  |  |  |  |
|  |  |  |  |  |  |  |
|  |  |  |  |  |  |  |
|  |  |  |  |  |  |  |
|  |  |  |  |  |  |  |
|  |  |  |  |  |  |  |

Total

# Purchase & Sales Tracker

DATES FROM _____

| Item | Purchase Date | Sale Date | Sale Website | Purchase Price | Sale Price | Profit |
|------|---------------|-----------|--------------|----------------|------------|--------|
|  |  |  |  |  |  |  |
|  |  |  |  |  |  |  |
|  |  |  |  |  |  |  |
|  |  |  |  |  |  |  |
|  |  |  |  |  |  |  |
|  |  |  |  |  |  |  |
|  |  |  |  |  |  |  |
|  |  |  |  |  |  |  |
|  |  |  |  |  |  |  |
|  |  |  |  |  |  |  |
|  |  |  |  |  |  |  |
|  |  |  |  |  |  |  |
|  |  |  |  |  |  |  |
|  |  |  |  |  |  |  |
|  |  |  |  |  |  |  |
|  |  |  |  |  |  |  |
|  |  |  |  |  |  |  |
|  |  |  |  |  |  |  |
|  |  |  |  |  |  |  |
|  |  |  |  |  |  |  |
|  |  |  |  |  |  |  |
|  |  |  |  |  |  |  |
|  |  |  |  |  |  |  |
|  |  |  |  |  |  |  |
|  |  |  |  |  |  |  |
|  |  |  |  |  |  |  |

Total

# Purchase & Sales Tracker

DATES FROM _____

| Item | Purchase Date | Sale Date | Sale Website | Purchase Price | Sale Price | Profit |
|------|---------------|-----------|--------------|----------------|------------|--------|
|  |  |  |  |  |  |  |
|  |  |  |  |  |  |  |
|  |  |  |  |  |  |  |
|  |  |  |  |  |  |  |
|  |  |  |  |  |  |  |
|  |  |  |  |  |  |  |
|  |  |  |  |  |  |  |
|  |  |  |  |  |  |  |
|  |  |  |  |  |  |  |
|  |  |  |  |  |  |  |
|  |  |  |  |  |  |  |
|  |  |  |  |  |  |  |
|  |  |  |  |  |  |  |
|  |  |  |  |  |  |  |
|  |  |  |  |  |  |  |
|  |  |  |  |  |  |  |
|  |  |  |  |  |  |  |
|  |  |  |  |  |  |  |
|  |  |  |  |  |  |  |
|  |  |  |  |  |  |  |
|  |  |  |  |  |  |  |
|  |  |  |  |  |  |  |
|  |  |  |  |  |  |  |
|  |  |  |  |  |  |  |
|  |  |  |  |  |  |  |
|  |  |  |  |  |  |  |
|  |  |  |  |  |  |  |

Total

# Purchase & Sales Tracker

DATES FROM _____

| Item | Purchase Date | Sale Date | Sale Website | Purchase Price | Sale Price | Profit |
|------|---------------|-----------|--------------|----------------|------------|--------|
|  |  |  |  |  |  |  |
|  |  |  |  |  |  |  |
|  |  |  |  |  |  |  |
|  |  |  |  |  |  |  |
|  |  |  |  |  |  |  |
|  |  |  |  |  |  |  |
|  |  |  |  |  |  |  |
|  |  |  |  |  |  |  |
|  |  |  |  |  |  |  |
|  |  |  |  |  |  |  |
|  |  |  |  |  |  |  |
|  |  |  |  |  |  |  |
|  |  |  |  |  |  |  |
|  |  |  |  |  |  |  |
|  |  |  |  |  |  |  |
|  |  |  |  |  |  |  |
|  |  |  |  |  |  |  |
|  |  |  |  |  |  |  |
|  |  |  |  |  |  |  |
|  |  |  |  |  |  |  |
|  |  |  |  |  |  |  |
|  |  |  |  |  |  |  |
|  |  |  |  |  |  |  |
|  |  |  |  |  |  |  |
|  |  |  |  |  |  |  |
|  |  |  |  |  |  |  |
|  |  |  |  |  |  |  |
|  |  |  |  |  |  |  |

Total

# Purchase & Sales Tracker

DATES FROM _____

| Item | Purchase Date | Sale Date | Sale Website | Purchase Price | Sale Price | Profit |
|------|---------------|-----------|--------------|----------------|------------|--------|
|  |  |  |  |  |  |  |
|  |  |  |  |  |  |  |
|  |  |  |  |  |  |  |
|  |  |  |  |  |  |  |
|  |  |  |  |  |  |  |
|  |  |  |  |  |  |  |
|  |  |  |  |  |  |  |
|  |  |  |  |  |  |  |
|  |  |  |  |  |  |  |
|  |  |  |  |  |  |  |
|  |  |  |  |  |  |  |
|  |  |  |  |  |  |  |
|  |  |  |  |  |  |  |
|  |  |  |  |  |  |  |
|  |  |  |  |  |  |  |
|  |  |  |  |  |  |  |
|  |  |  |  |  |  |  |
|  |  |  |  |  |  |  |
|  |  |  |  |  |  |  |
|  |  |  |  |  |  |  |
|  |  |  |  |  |  |  |
|  |  |  |  |  |  |  |
|  |  |  |  |  |  |  |
|  |  |  |  |  |  |  |
|  |  |  |  |  |  |  |
|  |  |  |  |  |  |  |
|  |  |  |  |  |  |  |
|  |  |  |  |  |  |  |

**Total**

# Purchase & Sales Tracker

DATES FROM _____

| Item | Purchase Date | Sale Date | Sale Website | Purchase Price | Sale Price | Profit |
|------|---------------|-----------|--------------|----------------|------------|--------|
|  |  |  |  |  |  |  |
|  |  |  |  |  |  |  |
|  |  |  |  |  |  |  |
|  |  |  |  |  |  |  |
|  |  |  |  |  |  |  |
|  |  |  |  |  |  |  |
|  |  |  |  |  |  |  |
|  |  |  |  |  |  |  |
|  |  |  |  |  |  |  |
|  |  |  |  |  |  |  |
|  |  |  |  |  |  |  |
|  |  |  |  |  |  |  |
|  |  |  |  |  |  |  |
|  |  |  |  |  |  |  |
|  |  |  |  |  |  |  |
|  |  |  |  |  |  |  |
|  |  |  |  |  |  |  |
|  |  |  |  |  |  |  |
|  |  |  |  |  |  |  |
|  |  |  |  |  |  |  |
|  |  |  |  |  |  |  |
|  |  |  |  |  |  |  |
|  |  |  |  |  |  |  |
|  |  |  |  |  |  |  |
|  |  |  |  |  |  |  |
|  |  |  |  |  |  |  |
|  |  |  |  |  |  |  |
|  |  |  |  |  |  |  |
|  |  |  |  |  |  |  |

Total

# Purchase & Sales Tracker

DATES FROM _____

| Item | Purchase Date | Sale Date | Sale Website | Purchase Price | Sale Price | Profit |
|------|---------------|-----------|--------------|----------------|------------|--------|
|      |               |           |              |                |            |        |
|      |               |           |              |                |            |        |
|      |               |           |              |                |            |        |
|      |               |           |              |                |            |        |
|      |               |           |              |                |            |        |
|      |               |           |              |                |            |        |
|      |               |           |              |                |            |        |
|      |               |           |              |                |            |        |
|      |               |           |              |                |            |        |
|      |               |           |              |                |            |        |
|      |               |           |              |                |            |        |
|      |               |           |              |                |            |        |
|      |               |           |              |                |            |        |
|      |               |           |              |                |            |        |
|      |               |           |              |                |            |        |
|      |               |           |              |                |            |        |
|      |               |           |              |                |            |        |
|      |               |           |              |                |            |        |
|      |               |           |              |                |            |        |
|      |               |           |              |                |            |        |
|      |               |           |              |                |            |        |
|      |               |           |              |                |            |        |
|      |               |           |              |                |            |        |
|      |               |           |              |                |            |        |
|      |               |           |              |                |            |        |
|      |               |           |              |                |            |        |

Total

# Purchase & Sales Tracker

| Item | Purchase Date | Sale Date | Sale Website | Purchase Price | Sale Price | Profit |
|---|---|---|---|---|---|---|
|  |  |  |  |  |  |  |
|  |  |  |  |  |  |  |
|  |  |  |  |  |  |  |
|  |  |  |  |  |  |  |
|  |  |  |  |  |  |  |
|  |  |  |  |  |  |  |
|  |  |  |  |  |  |  |
|  |  |  |  |  |  |  |
|  |  |  |  |  |  |  |
|  |  |  |  |  |  |  |
|  |  |  |  |  |  |  |
|  |  |  |  |  |  |  |
|  |  |  |  |  |  |  |
|  |  |  |  |  |  |  |
|  |  |  |  |  |  |  |
|  |  |  |  |  |  |  |
|  |  |  |  |  |  |  |
|  |  |  |  |  |  |  |
|  |  |  |  |  |  |  |
|  |  |  |  |  |  |  |
|  |  |  |  |  |  |  |
|  |  |  |  |  |  |  |
|  |  |  |  |  |  |  |
|  |  |  |  |  |  |  |
|  |  |  |  |  |  |  |
|  |  |  |  |  |  |  |
|  |  |  |  |  |  |  |
|  |  |  |  |  |  |  |

**Total**

# Purchase & Sales Tracker

DATES FROM _____

| Item | Purchase Date | Sale Date | Sale Website | Purchase Price | Sale Price | Profit |
|------|---------------|-----------|--------------|----------------|------------|--------|
|  |  |  |  |  |  |  |
|  |  |  |  |  |  |  |
|  |  |  |  |  |  |  |
|  |  |  |  |  |  |  |
|  |  |  |  |  |  |  |
|  |  |  |  |  |  |  |
|  |  |  |  |  |  |  |
|  |  |  |  |  |  |  |
|  |  |  |  |  |  |  |
|  |  |  |  |  |  |  |
|  |  |  |  |  |  |  |
|  |  |  |  |  |  |  |
|  |  |  |  |  |  |  |
|  |  |  |  |  |  |  |
|  |  |  |  |  |  |  |
|  |  |  |  |  |  |  |
|  |  |  |  |  |  |  |
|  |  |  |  |  |  |  |
|  |  |  |  |  |  |  |
|  |  |  |  |  |  |  |
|  |  |  |  |  |  |  |
|  |  |  |  |  |  |  |
|  |  |  |  |  |  |  |
|  |  |  |  |  |  |  |
|  |  |  |  |  |  |  |
|  |  |  |  |  |  |  |

Total

# Purchase & Sales Tracker

DATES FROM _____

| Item | Purchase Date | Sale Date | Sale Website | Purchase Price | Sale Price | Profit |
|---|---|---|---|---|---|---|
| | | | | | | |
| | | | | | | |
| | | | | | | |
| | | | | | | |
| | | | | | | |
| | | | | | | |
| | | | | | | |
| | | | | | | |
| | | | | | | |
| | | | | | | |
| | | | | | | |
| | | | | | | |
| | | | | | | |
| | | | | | | |
| | | | | | | |
| | | | | | | |
| | | | | | | |
| | | | | | | |
| | | | | | | |
| | | | | | | |
| | | | | | | |
| | | | | | | |
| | | | | | | |
| | | | | | | |
| | | | | | | |
| | | | | | | |
| | | | | | | |
| | | | | | | |

Total | | |

# Purchase & Sales Tracker

DATES FROM _____

| Item | Purchase Date | Sale Date | Sale Website | Purchase Price | Sale Price | Profit |
|------|---------------|-----------|--------------|----------------|------------|--------|
|  |  |  |  |  |  |  |
|  |  |  |  |  |  |  |
|  |  |  |  |  |  |  |
|  |  |  |  |  |  |  |
|  |  |  |  |  |  |  |
|  |  |  |  |  |  |  |
|  |  |  |  |  |  |  |
|  |  |  |  |  |  |  |
|  |  |  |  |  |  |  |
|  |  |  |  |  |  |  |
|  |  |  |  |  |  |  |
|  |  |  |  |  |  |  |
|  |  |  |  |  |  |  |
|  |  |  |  |  |  |  |
|  |  |  |  |  |  |  |
|  |  |  |  |  |  |  |
|  |  |  |  |  |  |  |
|  |  |  |  |  |  |  |
|  |  |  |  |  |  |  |
|  |  |  |  |  |  |  |
|  |  |  |  |  |  |  |
|  |  |  |  |  |  |  |
|  |  |  |  |  |  |  |
|  |  |  |  |  |  |  |
|  |  |  |  |  |  |  |
|  |  |  |  |  |  |  |
|  |  |  |  |  |  |  |
|  |  |  |  |  |  |  |

Total

# Purchase & Sales Tracker

DATES FROM _____

| Item | Purchase Date | Sale Date | Sale Website | Purchase Price | Sale Price | Profit |
|------|---------------|-----------|--------------|----------------|------------|--------|
|      |               |           |              |                |            |        |
|      |               |           |              |                |            |        |
|      |               |           |              |                |            |        |
|      |               |           |              |                |            |        |
|      |               |           |              |                |            |        |
|      |               |           |              |                |            |        |
|      |               |           |              |                |            |        |
|      |               |           |              |                |            |        |
|      |               |           |              |                |            |        |
|      |               |           |              |                |            |        |
|      |               |           |              |                |            |        |
|      |               |           |              |                |            |        |
|      |               |           |              |                |            |        |
|      |               |           |              |                |            |        |
|      |               |           |              |                |            |        |
|      |               |           |              |                |            |        |
|      |               |           |              |                |            |        |
|      |               |           |              |                |            |        |
|      |               |           |              |                |            |        |
|      |               |           |              |                |            |        |
|      |               |           |              |                |            |        |
|      |               |           |              |                |            |        |
|      |               |           |              |                |            |        |
|      |               |           |              |                |            |        |
|      |               |           |              |                |            |        |
|      |               |           |              |                |            |        |
|      |               |           |              |                |            |        |
|      |               |           |              |                |            |        |

Total

# Purchase & Sales Tracker

DATES FROM _____

| Item | Purchase Date | Sale Date | Sale Website | Purchase Price | Sale Price | Profit |
|------|---------------|-----------|--------------|----------------|------------|--------|
|      |               |           |              |                |            |        |
|      |               |           |              |                |            |        |
|      |               |           |              |                |            |        |
|      |               |           |              |                |            |        |
|      |               |           |              |                |            |        |
|      |               |           |              |                |            |        |
|      |               |           |              |                |            |        |
|      |               |           |              |                |            |        |
|      |               |           |              |                |            |        |
|      |               |           |              |                |            |        |
|      |               |           |              |                |            |        |
|      |               |           |              |                |            |        |
|      |               |           |              |                |            |        |
|      |               |           |              |                |            |        |
|      |               |           |              |                |            |        |
|      |               |           |              |                |            |        |
|      |               |           |              |                |            |        |
|      |               |           |              |                |            |        |
|      |               |           |              |                |            |        |
|      |               |           |              |                |            |        |
|      |               |           |              |                |            |        |
|      |               |           |              |                |            |        |
|      |               |           |              |                |            |        |
|      |               |           |              |                |            |        |
|      |               |           |              |                |            |        |
|      |               |           |              |                |            |        |
|      |               |           |              |                |            |        |

Total

# Purchase & Sales Tracker

DATES FROM _____

| Item | Purchase Date | Sale Date | Sale Website | Purchase Price | Sale Price | Profit |
|------|---------------|-----------|--------------|----------------|------------|--------|
|      |               |           |              |                |            |        |
|      |               |           |              |                |            |        |
|      |               |           |              |                |            |        |
|      |               |           |              |                |            |        |
|      |               |           |              |                |            |        |
|      |               |           |              |                |            |        |
|      |               |           |              |                |            |        |
|      |               |           |              |                |            |        |
|      |               |           |              |                |            |        |
|      |               |           |              |                |            |        |
|      |               |           |              |                |            |        |
|      |               |           |              |                |            |        |
|      |               |           |              |                |            |        |
|      |               |           |              |                |            |        |
|      |               |           |              |                |            |        |
|      |               |           |              |                |            |        |
|      |               |           |              |                |            |        |
|      |               |           |              |                |            |        |
|      |               |           |              |                |            |        |
|      |               |           |              |                |            |        |
|      |               |           |              |                |            |        |
|      |               |           |              |                |            |        |
|      |               |           |              |                |            |        |
|      |               |           |              |                |            |        |
|      |               |           |              |                |            |        |
|      |               |           |              |                |            |        |
|      |               |           |              |                |            |        |

Total

# Purchase & Sales Tracker

DATES FROM _____

| Item | Purchase Date | Sale Date | Sale Website | Purchase Price | Sale Price | Profit |
|------|---------------|-----------|--------------|----------------|------------|--------|
|      |               |           |              |                |            |        |
|      |               |           |              |                |            |        |
|      |               |           |              |                |            |        |
|      |               |           |              |                |            |        |
|      |               |           |              |                |            |        |
|      |               |           |              |                |            |        |
|      |               |           |              |                |            |        |
|      |               |           |              |                |            |        |
|      |               |           |              |                |            |        |
|      |               |           |              |                |            |        |
|      |               |           |              |                |            |        |
|      |               |           |              |                |            |        |
|      |               |           |              |                |            |        |
|      |               |           |              |                |            |        |
|      |               |           |              |                |            |        |
|      |               |           |              |                |            |        |
|      |               |           |              |                |            |        |
|      |               |           |              |                |            |        |
|      |               |           |              |                |            |        |
|      |               |           |              |                |            |        |
|      |               |           |              |                |            |        |
|      |               |           |              |                |            |        |
|      |               |           |              |                |            |        |
|      |               |           |              |                |            |        |
|      |               |           |              |                |            |        |
|      |               |           |              |                |            |        |

Total

# Purchase & Sales Tracker

DATES FROM _____

| Item | Purchase Date | Sale Date | Sale Website | Purchase Price | Sale Price | Profit |
|------|---------------|-----------|--------------|----------------|------------|--------|
|      |               |           |              |                |            |        |
|      |               |           |              |                |            |        |
|      |               |           |              |                |            |        |
|      |               |           |              |                |            |        |
|      |               |           |              |                |            |        |
|      |               |           |              |                |            |        |
|      |               |           |              |                |            |        |
|      |               |           |              |                |            |        |
|      |               |           |              |                |            |        |
|      |               |           |              |                |            |        |
|      |               |           |              |                |            |        |
|      |               |           |              |                |            |        |
|      |               |           |              |                |            |        |
|      |               |           |              |                |            |        |
|      |               |           |              |                |            |        |
|      |               |           |              |                |            |        |
|      |               |           |              |                |            |        |
|      |               |           |              |                |            |        |
|      |               |           |              |                |            |        |
|      |               |           |              |                |            |        |
|      |               |           |              |                |            |        |
|      |               |           |              |                |            |        |
|      |               |           |              |                |            |        |
|      |               |           |              |                |            |        |
|      |               |           |              |                |            |        |
|      |               |           |              |                |            |        |
|      |               |           |              |                |            |        |
|      |               |           |              |                |            |        |
|      |               |           |              |                |            |        |

Total

# Purchase & Sales Tracker

DATES FROM _____

| Item | Purchase Date | Sale Date | Sale Website | Purchase Price | Sale Price | Profit |
|---|---|---|---|---|---|---|
| | | | | | | |
| | | | | | | |
| | | | | | | |
| | | | | | | |
| | | | | | | |
| | | | | | | |
| | | | | | | |
| | | | | | | |
| | | | | | | |
| | | | | | | |
| | | | | | | |
| | | | | | | |
| | | | | | | |
| | | | | | | |
| | | | | | | |
| | | | | | | |
| | | | | | | |
| | | | | | | |
| | | | | | | |
| | | | | | | |
| | | | | | | |
| | | | | | | |
| | | | | | | |
| | | | | | | |
| | | | | | | |
| | | | | | | |
| | | | | | | |

Total

# Purchase & Sales Tracker

DATES FROM _____

| Item | Purchase Date | Sale Date | Sale Website | Purchase Price | Sale Price | Profit |
|------|---------------|-----------|--------------|----------------|------------|--------|
| | | | | | | |
| | | | | | | |
| | | | | | | |
| | | | | | | |
| | | | | | | |
| | | | | | | |
| | | | | | | |
| | | | | | | |
| | | | | | | |
| | | | | | | |
| | | | | | | |
| | | | | | | |
| | | | | | | |
| | | | | | | |
| | | | | | | |
| | | | | | | |
| | | | | | | |
| | | | | | | |
| | | | | | | |
| | | | | | | |
| | | | | | | |
| | | | | | | |
| | | | | | | |
| | | | | | | |
| | | | | | | |
| | | | | | | |
| | | | | | | |
| | | | | | | |

Total

# Purchase & Sales Tracker

DATES FROM _____

| Item | Purchase Date | Sale Date | Sale Website | Purchase Price | Sale Price | Profit |
|------|---------------|-----------|--------------|----------------|------------|--------|
|      |               |           |              |                |            |        |
|      |               |           |              |                |            |        |
|      |               |           |              |                |            |        |
|      |               |           |              |                |            |        |
|      |               |           |              |                |            |        |
|      |               |           |              |                |            |        |
|      |               |           |              |                |            |        |
|      |               |           |              |                |            |        |
|      |               |           |              |                |            |        |
|      |               |           |              |                |            |        |
|      |               |           |              |                |            |        |
|      |               |           |              |                |            |        |
|      |               |           |              |                |            |        |
|      |               |           |              |                |            |        |
|      |               |           |              |                |            |        |
|      |               |           |              |                |            |        |
|      |               |           |              |                |            |        |
|      |               |           |              |                |            |        |
|      |               |           |              |                |            |        |
|      |               |           |              |                |            |        |
|      |               |           |              |                |            |        |
|      |               |           |              |                |            |        |
|      |               |           |              |                |            |        |
|      |               |           |              |                |            |        |
|      |               |           |              |                |            |        |
|      |               |           |              |                |            |        |
|      |               |           |              |                |            |        |

Total

# Purchase & Sales Tracker

DATES FROM _____

| Item | Purchase Date | Sale Date | Sale Website | Purchase Price | Sale Price | Profit |
|---|---|---|---|---|---|---|
| | | | | | | |
| | | | | | | |
| | | | | | | |
| | | | | | | |
| | | | | | | |
| | | | | | | |
| | | | | | | |
| | | | | | | |
| | | | | | | |
| | | | | | | |
| | | | | | | |
| | | | | | | |
| | | | | | | |
| | | | | | | |
| | | | | | | |
| | | | | | | |
| | | | | | | |
| | | | | | | |
| | | | | | | |
| | | | | | | |
| | | | | | | |
| | | | | | | |
| | | | | | | |
| | | | | | | |
| | | | | | | |
| | | | | | | |
| | | | | | | |
| | | | | | | |

Total

# Purchase & Sales Tracker

DATES FROM _____

| Item | Purchase Date | Sale Date | Sale Website | Purchase Price | Sale Price | Profit |
|------|------|------|------|------|------|------|
| | | | | | | |
| | | | | | | |
| | | | | | | |
| | | | | | | |
| | | | | | | |
| | | | | | | |
| | | | | | | |
| | | | | | | |
| | | | | | | |
| | | | | | | |
| | | | | | | |
| | | | | | | |
| | | | | | | |
| | | | | | | |
| | | | | | | |
| | | | | | | |
| | | | | | | |
| | | | | | | |
| | | | | | | |
| | | | | | | |
| | | | | | | |
| | | | | | | |
| | | | | | | |
| | | | | | | |
| | | | | | | |
| | | | | | | |
| | | | | | | |

**Total**

# Purchase & Sales Tracker

DATES FROM _____

| Item | Purchase Date | Sale Date | Sale Website | Purchase Price | Sale Price | Profit |
|------|---------------|-----------|--------------|----------------|------------|--------|
|  |  |  |  |  |  |  |
|  |  |  |  |  |  |  |
|  |  |  |  |  |  |  |
|  |  |  |  |  |  |  |
|  |  |  |  |  |  |  |
|  |  |  |  |  |  |  |
|  |  |  |  |  |  |  |
|  |  |  |  |  |  |  |
|  |  |  |  |  |  |  |
|  |  |  |  |  |  |  |
|  |  |  |  |  |  |  |
|  |  |  |  |  |  |  |
|  |  |  |  |  |  |  |
|  |  |  |  |  |  |  |
|  |  |  |  |  |  |  |
|  |  |  |  |  |  |  |
|  |  |  |  |  |  |  |
|  |  |  |  |  |  |  |
|  |  |  |  |  |  |  |
|  |  |  |  |  |  |  |
|  |  |  |  |  |  |  |
|  |  |  |  |  |  |  |
|  |  |  |  |  |  |  |
|  |  |  |  |  |  |  |
|  |  |  |  |  |  |  |
|  |  |  |  |  |  |  |
|  |  |  |  |  |  |  |
|  |  |  |  |  |  |  |

**Total**

# Purchase & Sales Tracker

DATES FROM _____

| Item | Purchase Date | Sale Date | Sale Website | Purchase Price | Sale Price | Profit |
|------|---------------|-----------|--------------|----------------|------------|--------|
|      |               |           |              |                |            |        |
|      |               |           |              |                |            |        |
|      |               |           |              |                |            |        |
|      |               |           |              |                |            |        |
|      |               |           |              |                |            |        |
|      |               |           |              |                |            |        |
|      |               |           |              |                |            |        |
|      |               |           |              |                |            |        |
|      |               |           |              |                |            |        |
|      |               |           |              |                |            |        |
|      |               |           |              |                |            |        |
|      |               |           |              |                |            |        |
|      |               |           |              |                |            |        |
|      |               |           |              |                |            |        |
|      |               |           |              |                |            |        |
|      |               |           |              |                |            |        |
|      |               |           |              |                |            |        |
|      |               |           |              |                |            |        |
|      |               |           |              |                |            |        |
|      |               |           |              |                |            |        |
|      |               |           |              |                |            |        |
|      |               |           |              |                |            |        |
|      |               |           |              |                |            |        |
|      |               |           |              |                |            |        |
|      |               |           |              |                |            |        |
|      |               |           |              |                |            |        |
|      |               |           |              |                |            |        |
|      |               |           |              |                |            |        |

Total

# Purchase & Sales Tracker

DATES FROM _____

| Item | Purchase Date | Sale Date | Sale Website | Purchase Price | Sale Price | Profit |
|------|---------------|-----------|--------------|----------------|------------|--------|
|      |               |           |              |                |            |        |
|      |               |           |              |                |            |        |
|      |               |           |              |                |            |        |
|      |               |           |              |                |            |        |
|      |               |           |              |                |            |        |
|      |               |           |              |                |            |        |
|      |               |           |              |                |            |        |
|      |               |           |              |                |            |        |
|      |               |           |              |                |            |        |
|      |               |           |              |                |            |        |
|      |               |           |              |                |            |        |
|      |               |           |              |                |            |        |
|      |               |           |              |                |            |        |
|      |               |           |              |                |            |        |
|      |               |           |              |                |            |        |
|      |               |           |              |                |            |        |
|      |               |           |              |                |            |        |
|      |               |           |              |                |            |        |
|      |               |           |              |                |            |        |
|      |               |           |              |                |            |        |
|      |               |           |              |                |            |        |
|      |               |           |              |                |            |        |
|      |               |           |              |                |            |        |
|      |               |           |              |                |            |        |
|      |               |           |              |                |            |        |
|      |               |           |              |                |            |        |
|      |               |           |              |                |            |        |

Total

# Purchase & Sales Tracker

DATES FROM _____

| Item | Purchase Date | Sale Date | Sale Website | Purchase Price | Sale Price | Profit |
|------|---------------|-----------|--------------|----------------|------------|--------|
|  |  |  |  |  |  |  |
|  |  |  |  |  |  |  |
|  |  |  |  |  |  |  |
|  |  |  |  |  |  |  |
|  |  |  |  |  |  |  |
|  |  |  |  |  |  |  |
|  |  |  |  |  |  |  |
|  |  |  |  |  |  |  |
|  |  |  |  |  |  |  |
|  |  |  |  |  |  |  |
|  |  |  |  |  |  |  |
|  |  |  |  |  |  |  |
|  |  |  |  |  |  |  |
|  |  |  |  |  |  |  |
|  |  |  |  |  |  |  |
|  |  |  |  |  |  |  |
|  |  |  |  |  |  |  |
|  |  |  |  |  |  |  |
|  |  |  |  |  |  |  |
|  |  |  |  |  |  |  |
|  |  |  |  |  |  |  |
|  |  |  |  |  |  |  |
|  |  |  |  |  |  |  |
|  |  |  |  |  |  |  |
|  |  |  |  |  |  |  |
|  |  |  |  |  |  |  |
|  |  |  |  |  |  |  |

Total

# Purchase & Sales Tracker

DATES FROM _____

| Item | Purchase Date | Sale Date | Sale Website | Purchase Price | Sale Price | Profit |
|---|---|---|---|---|---|---|
|  |  |  |  |  |  |  |
|  |  |  |  |  |  |  |
|  |  |  |  |  |  |  |
|  |  |  |  |  |  |  |
|  |  |  |  |  |  |  |
|  |  |  |  |  |  |  |
|  |  |  |  |  |  |  |
|  |  |  |  |  |  |  |
|  |  |  |  |  |  |  |
|  |  |  |  |  |  |  |
|  |  |  |  |  |  |  |
|  |  |  |  |  |  |  |
|  |  |  |  |  |  |  |
|  |  |  |  |  |  |  |
|  |  |  |  |  |  |  |
|  |  |  |  |  |  |  |
|  |  |  |  |  |  |  |
|  |  |  |  |  |  |  |
|  |  |  |  |  |  |  |
|  |  |  |  |  |  |  |
|  |  |  |  |  |  |  |
|  |  |  |  |  |  |  |
|  |  |  |  |  |  |  |
|  |  |  |  |  |  |  |
|  |  |  |  |  |  |  |
|  |  |  |  |  |  |  |
|  |  |  |  |  |  |  |
|  |  |  |  |  |  |  |
|  |  |  |  |  |  |  |
|  |  |  |  |  |  |  |

Total

# Purchase & Sales Tracker

DATES FROM _____

| Item | Purchase Date | Sale Date | Sale Website | Purchase Price | Sale Price | Profit |
|------|---------------|-----------|--------------|----------------|------------|--------|
|  |  |  |  |  |  |  |
|  |  |  |  |  |  |  |
|  |  |  |  |  |  |  |
|  |  |  |  |  |  |  |
|  |  |  |  |  |  |  |
|  |  |  |  |  |  |  |
|  |  |  |  |  |  |  |
|  |  |  |  |  |  |  |
|  |  |  |  |  |  |  |
|  |  |  |  |  |  |  |
|  |  |  |  |  |  |  |
|  |  |  |  |  |  |  |
|  |  |  |  |  |  |  |
|  |  |  |  |  |  |  |
|  |  |  |  |  |  |  |
|  |  |  |  |  |  |  |
|  |  |  |  |  |  |  |
|  |  |  |  |  |  |  |
|  |  |  |  |  |  |  |
|  |  |  |  |  |  |  |
|  |  |  |  |  |  |  |
|  |  |  |  |  |  |  |
|  |  |  |  |  |  |  |
|  |  |  |  |  |  |  |
|  |  |  |  |  |  |  |
|  |  |  |  |  |  |  |
|  |  |  |  |  |  |  |

Total

# Purchase & Sales Tracker

DATES FROM _____

| Item | Purchase Date | Sale Date | Sale Website | Purchase Price | Sale Price | Profit |
|------|---------------|-----------|--------------|----------------|------------|--------|
|  |  |  |  |  |  |  |
|  |  |  |  |  |  |  |
|  |  |  |  |  |  |  |
|  |  |  |  |  |  |  |
|  |  |  |  |  |  |  |
|  |  |  |  |  |  |  |
|  |  |  |  |  |  |  |
|  |  |  |  |  |  |  |
|  |  |  |  |  |  |  |
|  |  |  |  |  |  |  |
|  |  |  |  |  |  |  |
|  |  |  |  |  |  |  |
|  |  |  |  |  |  |  |
|  |  |  |  |  |  |  |
|  |  |  |  |  |  |  |
|  |  |  |  |  |  |  |
|  |  |  |  |  |  |  |
|  |  |  |  |  |  |  |
|  |  |  |  |  |  |  |
|  |  |  |  |  |  |  |
|  |  |  |  |  |  |  |
|  |  |  |  |  |  |  |
|  |  |  |  |  |  |  |
|  |  |  |  |  |  |  |
|  |  |  |  |  |  |  |
|  |  |  |  |  |  |  |
|  |  |  |  |  |  |  |
|  |  |  |  |  |  |  |

Total

# Purchase & Sales Tracker

DATES FROM _____

| Item | Purchase Date | Sale Date | Sale Website | Purchase Price | Sale Price | Profit |
|---|---|---|---|---|---|---|
|  |  |  |  |  |  |  |
|  |  |  |  |  |  |  |
|  |  |  |  |  |  |  |
|  |  |  |  |  |  |  |
|  |  |  |  |  |  |  |
|  |  |  |  |  |  |  |
|  |  |  |  |  |  |  |
|  |  |  |  |  |  |  |
|  |  |  |  |  |  |  |
|  |  |  |  |  |  |  |
|  |  |  |  |  |  |  |
|  |  |  |  |  |  |  |
|  |  |  |  |  |  |  |
|  |  |  |  |  |  |  |
|  |  |  |  |  |  |  |
|  |  |  |  |  |  |  |
|  |  |  |  |  |  |  |
|  |  |  |  |  |  |  |
|  |  |  |  |  |  |  |
|  |  |  |  |  |  |  |
|  |  |  |  |  |  |  |
|  |  |  |  |  |  |  |
|  |  |  |  |  |  |  |
|  |  |  |  |  |  |  |
|  |  |  |  |  |  |  |
|  |  |  |  |  |  |  |

Total

# Purchase & Sales Tracker

DATES FROM _____

| Item | Purchase Date | Sale Date | Sale Website | Purchase Price | Sale Price | Profit |
|------|---------------|-----------|--------------|----------------|------------|--------|
|  |  |  |  |  |  |  |
|  |  |  |  |  |  |  |
|  |  |  |  |  |  |  |
|  |  |  |  |  |  |  |
|  |  |  |  |  |  |  |
|  |  |  |  |  |  |  |
|  |  |  |  |  |  |  |
|  |  |  |  |  |  |  |
|  |  |  |  |  |  |  |
|  |  |  |  |  |  |  |
|  |  |  |  |  |  |  |
|  |  |  |  |  |  |  |
|  |  |  |  |  |  |  |
|  |  |  |  |  |  |  |
|  |  |  |  |  |  |  |
|  |  |  |  |  |  |  |
|  |  |  |  |  |  |  |
|  |  |  |  |  |  |  |
|  |  |  |  |  |  |  |
|  |  |  |  |  |  |  |
|  |  |  |  |  |  |  |
|  |  |  |  |  |  |  |
|  |  |  |  |  |  |  |
|  |  |  |  |  |  |  |
|  |  |  |  |  |  |  |
|  |  |  |  |  |  |  |
|  |  |  |  |  |  |  |
|  |  |  |  |  |  |  |
|  |  |  |  |  |  |  |

Total

# Purchase & Sales Tracker

DATES FROM _____

| Item | Purchase Date | Sale Date | Sale Website | Purchase Price | Sale Price | Profit |
|------|---------------|-----------|--------------|----------------|------------|--------|
|  |  |  |  |  |  |  |
|  |  |  |  |  |  |  |
|  |  |  |  |  |  |  |
|  |  |  |  |  |  |  |
|  |  |  |  |  |  |  |
|  |  |  |  |  |  |  |
|  |  |  |  |  |  |  |
|  |  |  |  |  |  |  |
|  |  |  |  |  |  |  |
|  |  |  |  |  |  |  |
|  |  |  |  |  |  |  |
|  |  |  |  |  |  |  |
|  |  |  |  |  |  |  |
|  |  |  |  |  |  |  |
|  |  |  |  |  |  |  |
|  |  |  |  |  |  |  |
|  |  |  |  |  |  |  |
|  |  |  |  |  |  |  |
|  |  |  |  |  |  |  |
|  |  |  |  |  |  |  |
|  |  |  |  |  |  |  |
|  |  |  |  |  |  |  |
|  |  |  |  |  |  |  |
|  |  |  |  |  |  |  |
|  |  |  |  |  |  |  |
|  |  |  |  |  |  |  |

Total | | | |

# Purchase & Sales Tracker

DATES FROM _____

| Item | Purchase Date | Sale Date | Sale Website | Purchase Price | Sale Price | Profit |
|------|---------------|-----------|--------------|----------------|------------|--------|
| | | | | | | |
| | | | | | | |
| | | | | | | |
| | | | | | | |
| | | | | | | |
| | | | | | | |
| | | | | | | |
| | | | | | | |
| | | | | | | |
| | | | | | | |
| | | | | | | |
| | | | | | | |
| | | | | | | |
| | | | | | | |
| | | | | | | |
| | | | | | | |
| | | | | | | |
| | | | | | | |
| | | | | | | |
| | | | | | | |
| | | | | | | |
| | | | | | | |
| | | | | | | |
| | | | | | | |
| | | | | | | |
| | | | | | | |
| | | | | | | |
| | | | | | | |

Total

# Purchase & Sales Tracker

DATES FROM _____

| Item | Purchase Date | Sale Date | Sale Website | Purchase Price | Sale Price | Profit |
|------|---------------|-----------|--------------|----------------|------------|--------|
|  |  |  |  |  |  |  |
|  |  |  |  |  |  |  |
|  |  |  |  |  |  |  |
|  |  |  |  |  |  |  |
|  |  |  |  |  |  |  |
|  |  |  |  |  |  |  |
|  |  |  |  |  |  |  |
|  |  |  |  |  |  |  |
|  |  |  |  |  |  |  |
|  |  |  |  |  |  |  |
|  |  |  |  |  |  |  |
|  |  |  |  |  |  |  |
|  |  |  |  |  |  |  |
|  |  |  |  |  |  |  |
|  |  |  |  |  |  |  |
|  |  |  |  |  |  |  |
|  |  |  |  |  |  |  |
|  |  |  |  |  |  |  |
|  |  |  |  |  |  |  |
|  |  |  |  |  |  |  |
|  |  |  |  |  |  |  |
|  |  |  |  |  |  |  |
|  |  |  |  |  |  |  |
|  |  |  |  |  |  |  |
|  |  |  |  |  |  |  |
|  |  |  |  |  |  |  |
|  |  |  |  |  |  |  |

Total

# Purchase & Sales Tracker

DATES FROM _____

| Item | Purchase Date | Sale Date | Sale Website | Purchase Price | Sale Price | Profit |
|------|--------------|-----------|--------------|----------------|------------|--------|
| | | | | | | |
| | | | | | | |
| | | | | | | |
| | | | | | | |
| | | | | | | |
| | | | | | | |
| | | | | | | |
| | | | | | | |
| | | | | | | |
| | | | | | | |
| | | | | | | |
| | | | | | | |
| | | | | | | |
| | | | | | | |
| | | | | | | |
| | | | | | | |
| | | | | | | |
| | | | | | | |
| | | | | | | |
| | | | | | | |
| | | | | | | |
| | | | | | | |
| | | | | | | |
| | | | | | | |
| | | | | | | |
| | | | | | | |

Total

# Purchase & Sales Tracker

DATES FROM _____

| Item | Purchase Date | Sale Date | Sale Website | Purchase Price | Sale Price | Profit |
|------|---------------|-----------|--------------|----------------|------------|--------|
|      |               |           |              |                |            |        |
|      |               |           |              |                |            |        |
|      |               |           |              |                |            |        |
|      |               |           |              |                |            |        |
|      |               |           |              |                |            |        |
|      |               |           |              |                |            |        |
|      |               |           |              |                |            |        |
|      |               |           |              |                |            |        |
|      |               |           |              |                |            |        |
|      |               |           |              |                |            |        |
|      |               |           |              |                |            |        |
|      |               |           |              |                |            |        |
|      |               |           |              |                |            |        |
|      |               |           |              |                |            |        |
|      |               |           |              |                |            |        |
|      |               |           |              |                |            |        |
|      |               |           |              |                |            |        |
|      |               |           |              |                |            |        |
|      |               |           |              |                |            |        |
|      |               |           |              |                |            |        |
|      |               |           |              |                |            |        |
|      |               |           |              |                |            |        |
|      |               |           |              |                |            |        |
|      |               |           |              |                |            |        |
|      |               |           |              |                |            |        |
|      |               |           |              |                |            |        |
|      |               |           |              |                |            |        |
|      |               |           |              |                |            |        |
|      |               |           |              |                |            |        |

Total

# Purchase & Sales Tracker

DATES FROM _____

| Item | Purchase Date | Sale Date | Sale Website | Purchase Price | Sale Price | Profit |
|------|---------------|-----------|--------------|----------------|------------|--------|
|  |  |  |  |  |  |  |
|  |  |  |  |  |  |  |
|  |  |  |  |  |  |  |
|  |  |  |  |  |  |  |
|  |  |  |  |  |  |  |
|  |  |  |  |  |  |  |
|  |  |  |  |  |  |  |
|  |  |  |  |  |  |  |
|  |  |  |  |  |  |  |
|  |  |  |  |  |  |  |
|  |  |  |  |  |  |  |
|  |  |  |  |  |  |  |
|  |  |  |  |  |  |  |
|  |  |  |  |  |  |  |
|  |  |  |  |  |  |  |
|  |  |  |  |  |  |  |
|  |  |  |  |  |  |  |
|  |  |  |  |  |  |  |
|  |  |  |  |  |  |  |
|  |  |  |  |  |  |  |
|  |  |  |  |  |  |  |
|  |  |  |  |  |  |  |
|  |  |  |  |  |  |  |
|  |  |  |  |  |  |  |
|  |  |  |  |  |  |  |
|  |  |  |  |  |  |  |
|  |  |  |  |  |  |  |
|  |  |  |  |  |  |  |

Total

# Purchase & Sales Tracker

DATES FROM _____

| Item | Purchase Date | Sale Date | Sale Website | Purchase Price | Sale Price | Profit |
|------|---------------|-----------|--------------|----------------|------------|--------|
|      |               |           |              |                |            |        |
|      |               |           |              |                |            |        |
|      |               |           |              |                |            |        |
|      |               |           |              |                |            |        |
|      |               |           |              |                |            |        |
|      |               |           |              |                |            |        |
|      |               |           |              |                |            |        |
|      |               |           |              |                |            |        |
|      |               |           |              |                |            |        |
|      |               |           |              |                |            |        |
|      |               |           |              |                |            |        |
|      |               |           |              |                |            |        |
|      |               |           |              |                |            |        |
|      |               |           |              |                |            |        |
|      |               |           |              |                |            |        |
|      |               |           |              |                |            |        |
|      |               |           |              |                |            |        |
|      |               |           |              |                |            |        |
|      |               |           |              |                |            |        |
|      |               |           |              |                |            |        |
|      |               |           |              |                |            |        |
|      |               |           |              |                |            |        |
|      |               |           |              |                |            |        |
|      |               |           |              |                |            |        |
|      |               |           |              |                |            |        |
|      |               |           |              |                |            |        |
|      |               |           |              |                |            |        |

Total

# Purchase & Sales Tracker

DATES FROM _____

| Item | Purchase Date | Sale Date | Sale Website | Purchase Price | Sale Price | Profit |
|------|---------------|-----------|--------------|----------------|------------|--------|
| | | | | | | |
| | | | | | | |
| | | | | | | |
| | | | | | | |
| | | | | | | |
| | | | | | | |
| | | | | | | |
| | | | | | | |
| | | | | | | |
| | | | | | | |
| | | | | | | |
| | | | | | | |
| | | | | | | |
| | | | | | | |
| | | | | | | |
| | | | | | | |
| | | | | | | |
| | | | | | | |
| | | | | | | |
| | | | | | | |
| | | | | | | |
| | | | | | | |
| | | | | | | |
| | | | | | | |
| | | | | | | |
| | | | | | | |
| | | | | | | |

Total

# Purchase & Sales Tracker

DATES FROM _____

| Item | Purchase Date | Sale Date | Sale Website | Purchase Price | Sale Price | Profit |
|------|---------------|-----------|--------------|----------------|------------|--------|
|  |  |  |  |  |  |  |
|  |  |  |  |  |  |  |
|  |  |  |  |  |  |  |
|  |  |  |  |  |  |  |
|  |  |  |  |  |  |  |
|  |  |  |  |  |  |  |
|  |  |  |  |  |  |  |
|  |  |  |  |  |  |  |
|  |  |  |  |  |  |  |
|  |  |  |  |  |  |  |
|  |  |  |  |  |  |  |
|  |  |  |  |  |  |  |
|  |  |  |  |  |  |  |
|  |  |  |  |  |  |  |
|  |  |  |  |  |  |  |
|  |  |  |  |  |  |  |
|  |  |  |  |  |  |  |
|  |  |  |  |  |  |  |
|  |  |  |  |  |  |  |
|  |  |  |  |  |  |  |
|  |  |  |  |  |  |  |
|  |  |  |  |  |  |  |
|  |  |  |  |  |  |  |
|  |  |  |  |  |  |  |
|  |  |  |  |  |  |  |
|  |  |  |  |  |  |  |
|  |  |  |  |  |  |  |

Total

# Purchase & Sales Tracker

DATES FROM _____

| Item | Purchase Date | Sale Date | Sale Website | Purchase Price | Sale Price | Profit |
|------|---------------|-----------|--------------|----------------|------------|--------|
|      |               |           |              |                |            |        |
|      |               |           |              |                |            |        |
|      |               |           |              |                |            |        |
|      |               |           |              |                |            |        |
|      |               |           |              |                |            |        |
|      |               |           |              |                |            |        |
|      |               |           |              |                |            |        |
|      |               |           |              |                |            |        |
|      |               |           |              |                |            |        |
|      |               |           |              |                |            |        |
|      |               |           |              |                |            |        |
|      |               |           |              |                |            |        |
|      |               |           |              |                |            |        |
|      |               |           |              |                |            |        |
|      |               |           |              |                |            |        |
|      |               |           |              |                |            |        |
|      |               |           |              |                |            |        |
|      |               |           |              |                |            |        |
|      |               |           |              |                |            |        |
|      |               |           |              |                |            |        |
|      |               |           |              |                |            |        |
|      |               |           |              |                |            |        |
|      |               |           |              |                |            |        |
|      |               |           |              |                |            |        |
|      |               |           |              |                |            |        |
|      |               |           |              |                |            |        |
|      |               |           |              |                |            |        |

Total

# Purchase & Sales Tracker

DATES FROM _____

| Item | Purchase Date | Sale Date | Sale Website | Purchase Price | Sale Price | Profit |
|---|---|---|---|---|---|---|
| | | | | | | |
| | | | | | | |
| | | | | | | |
| | | | | | | |
| | | | | | | |
| | | | | | | |
| | | | | | | |
| | | | | | | |
| | | | | | | |
| | | | | | | |
| | | | | | | |
| | | | | | | |
| | | | | | | |
| | | | | | | |
| | | | | | | |
| | | | | | | |
| | | | | | | |
| | | | | | | |
| | | | | | | |
| | | | | | | |
| | | | | | | |
| | | | | | | |
| | | | | | | |
| | | | | | | |
| | | | | | | |
| | | | | | | |

Total

# Purchase & Sales Tracker

DATES FROM _____

| Item | Purchase Date | Sale Date | Sale Website | Purchase Price | Sale Price | Profit |
|------|---------------|-----------|--------------|----------------|------------|--------|
|      |               |           |              |                |            |        |
|      |               |           |              |                |            |        |
|      |               |           |              |                |            |        |
|      |               |           |              |                |            |        |
|      |               |           |              |                |            |        |
|      |               |           |              |                |            |        |
|      |               |           |              |                |            |        |
|      |               |           |              |                |            |        |
|      |               |           |              |                |            |        |
|      |               |           |              |                |            |        |
|      |               |           |              |                |            |        |
|      |               |           |              |                |            |        |
|      |               |           |              |                |            |        |
|      |               |           |              |                |            |        |
|      |               |           |              |                |            |        |
|      |               |           |              |                |            |        |
|      |               |           |              |                |            |        |
|      |               |           |              |                |            |        |
|      |               |           |              |                |            |        |
|      |               |           |              |                |            |        |
|      |               |           |              |                |            |        |
|      |               |           |              |                |            |        |
|      |               |           |              |                |            |        |
|      |               |           |              |                |            |        |
|      |               |           |              |                |            |        |
|      |               |           |              |                |            |        |
|      |               |           |              |                |            |        |

Total

# Purchase & Sales Tracker

DATES FROM _____

| Item | Purchase Date | Sale Date | Sale Website | Purchase Price | Sale Price | Profit |
|---|---|---|---|---|---|---|
|  |  |  |  |  |  |  |
|  |  |  |  |  |  |  |
|  |  |  |  |  |  |  |
|  |  |  |  |  |  |  |
|  |  |  |  |  |  |  |
|  |  |  |  |  |  |  |
|  |  |  |  |  |  |  |
|  |  |  |  |  |  |  |
|  |  |  |  |  |  |  |
|  |  |  |  |  |  |  |
|  |  |  |  |  |  |  |
|  |  |  |  |  |  |  |
|  |  |  |  |  |  |  |
|  |  |  |  |  |  |  |
|  |  |  |  |  |  |  |
|  |  |  |  |  |  |  |
|  |  |  |  |  |  |  |
|  |  |  |  |  |  |  |
|  |  |  |  |  |  |  |
|  |  |  |  |  |  |  |
|  |  |  |  |  |  |  |
|  |  |  |  |  |  |  |
|  |  |  |  |  |  |  |
|  |  |  |  |  |  |  |
|  |  |  |  |  |  |  |
|  |  |  |  |  |  |  |
|  |  |  |  |  |  |  |
|  |  |  |  |  |  |  |

Total

# Purchase & Sales Tracker

DATES FROM _____

| Item | Purchase Date | Sale Date | Sale Website | Purchase Price | Sale Price | Profit |
|---|---|---|---|---|---|---|
| | | | | | | |
| | | | | | | |
| | | | | | | |
| | | | | | | |
| | | | | | | |
| | | | | | | |
| | | | | | | |
| | | | | | | |
| | | | | | | |
| | | | | | | |
| | | | | | | |
| | | | | | | |
| | | | | | | |
| | | | | | | |
| | | | | | | |
| | | | | | | |
| | | | | | | |
| | | | | | | |
| | | | | | | |
| | | | | | | |
| | | | | | | |
| | | | | | | |
| | | | | | | |
| | | | | | | |
| | | | | | | |
| | | | | | | |
| | | | | | | |
| | | | | | | |
| | | | | | | |

Total

# Purchase & Sales Tracker

DATES FROM _____

| Item | Purchase Date | Sale Date | Sale Website | Purchase Price | Sale Price | Profit |
|------|---------------|-----------|--------------|----------------|------------|--------|
|  |  |  |  |  |  |  |
|  |  |  |  |  |  |  |
|  |  |  |  |  |  |  |
|  |  |  |  |  |  |  |
|  |  |  |  |  |  |  |
|  |  |  |  |  |  |  |
|  |  |  |  |  |  |  |
|  |  |  |  |  |  |  |
|  |  |  |  |  |  |  |
|  |  |  |  |  |  |  |
|  |  |  |  |  |  |  |
|  |  |  |  |  |  |  |
|  |  |  |  |  |  |  |
|  |  |  |  |  |  |  |
|  |  |  |  |  |  |  |
|  |  |  |  |  |  |  |
|  |  |  |  |  |  |  |
|  |  |  |  |  |  |  |
|  |  |  |  |  |  |  |
|  |  |  |  |  |  |  |
|  |  |  |  |  |  |  |
|  |  |  |  |  |  |  |
|  |  |  |  |  |  |  |
|  |  |  |  |  |  |  |
|  |  |  |  |  |  |  |
|  |  |  |  |  |  |  |

Total

# Purchase & Sales Tracker

DATES FROM _____

| Item | Purchase Date | Sale Date | Sale Website | Purchase Price | Sale Price | Profit |
|------|---------------|-----------|--------------|----------------|------------|--------|
|  |  |  |  |  |  |  |
|  |  |  |  |  |  |  |
|  |  |  |  |  |  |  |
|  |  |  |  |  |  |  |
|  |  |  |  |  |  |  |
|  |  |  |  |  |  |  |
|  |  |  |  |  |  |  |
|  |  |  |  |  |  |  |
|  |  |  |  |  |  |  |
|  |  |  |  |  |  |  |
|  |  |  |  |  |  |  |
|  |  |  |  |  |  |  |
|  |  |  |  |  |  |  |
|  |  |  |  |  |  |  |
|  |  |  |  |  |  |  |
|  |  |  |  |  |  |  |
|  |  |  |  |  |  |  |
|  |  |  |  |  |  |  |
|  |  |  |  |  |  |  |
|  |  |  |  |  |  |  |
|  |  |  |  |  |  |  |
|  |  |  |  |  |  |  |
|  |  |  |  |  |  |  |
|  |  |  |  |  |  |  |
|  |  |  |  |  |  |  |
|  |  |  |  |  |  |  |

Total

# Purchase & Sales Tracker

DATES FROM _____

| Item | Purchase Date | Sale Date | Sale Website | Purchase Price | Sale Price | Profit |
|------|---------------|-----------|--------------|----------------|------------|--------|
|      |               |           |              |                |            |        |
|      |               |           |              |                |            |        |
|      |               |           |              |                |            |        |
|      |               |           |              |                |            |        |
|      |               |           |              |                |            |        |
|      |               |           |              |                |            |        |
|      |               |           |              |                |            |        |
|      |               |           |              |                |            |        |
|      |               |           |              |                |            |        |
|      |               |           |              |                |            |        |
|      |               |           |              |                |            |        |
|      |               |           |              |                |            |        |
|      |               |           |              |                |            |        |
|      |               |           |              |                |            |        |
|      |               |           |              |                |            |        |
|      |               |           |              |                |            |        |
|      |               |           |              |                |            |        |
|      |               |           |              |                |            |        |
|      |               |           |              |                |            |        |
|      |               |           |              |                |            |        |
|      |               |           |              |                |            |        |
|      |               |           |              |                |            |        |
|      |               |           |              |                |            |        |
|      |               |           |              |                |            |        |
|      |               |           |              |                |            |        |
|      |               |           |              |                |            |        |

Total

# Purchase & Sales Tracker

| Item | Purchase Date | Sale Date | Sale Website | Purchase Price | Sale Price | Profit |
|------|---------------|-----------|--------------|----------------|------------|--------|
|  |  |  |  |  |  |  |
|  |  |  |  |  |  |  |
|  |  |  |  |  |  |  |
|  |  |  |  |  |  |  |
|  |  |  |  |  |  |  |
|  |  |  |  |  |  |  |
|  |  |  |  |  |  |  |
|  |  |  |  |  |  |  |
|  |  |  |  |  |  |  |
|  |  |  |  |  |  |  |
|  |  |  |  |  |  |  |
|  |  |  |  |  |  |  |
|  |  |  |  |  |  |  |
|  |  |  |  |  |  |  |
|  |  |  |  |  |  |  |
|  |  |  |  |  |  |  |
|  |  |  |  |  |  |  |
|  |  |  |  |  |  |  |
|  |  |  |  |  |  |  |
|  |  |  |  |  |  |  |
|  |  |  |  |  |  |  |
|  |  |  |  |  |  |  |
|  |  |  |  |  |  |  |
|  |  |  |  |  |  |  |
|  |  |  |  |  |  |  |
|  |  |  |  |  |  |  |
|  |  |  |  |  |  |  |
|  |  |  |  |  |  |  |
|  |  |  |  |  |  |  |

Total

# Purchase & Sales Tracker

DATES FROM _____

| Item | Purchase Date | Sale Date | Sale Website | Purchase Price | Sale Price | Profit |
|------|---------------|-----------|--------------|----------------|------------|--------|
|      |               |           |              |                |            |        |
|      |               |           |              |                |            |        |
|      |               |           |              |                |            |        |
|      |               |           |              |                |            |        |
|      |               |           |              |                |            |        |
|      |               |           |              |                |            |        |
|      |               |           |              |                |            |        |
|      |               |           |              |                |            |        |
|      |               |           |              |                |            |        |
|      |               |           |              |                |            |        |
|      |               |           |              |                |            |        |
|      |               |           |              |                |            |        |
|      |               |           |              |                |            |        |
|      |               |           |              |                |            |        |
|      |               |           |              |                |            |        |
|      |               |           |              |                |            |        |
|      |               |           |              |                |            |        |
|      |               |           |              |                |            |        |
|      |               |           |              |                |            |        |
|      |               |           |              |                |            |        |
|      |               |           |              |                |            |        |
|      |               |           |              |                |            |        |
|      |               |           |              |                |            |        |
|      |               |           |              |                |            |        |
|      |               |           |              |                |            |        |
|      |               |           |              |                |            |        |

Total

# Purchase & Sales Tracker

DATES FROM _____

| Item | Purchase Date | Sale Date | Sale Website | Purchase Price | Sale Price | Profit |
|------|---------------|-----------|--------------|----------------|------------|--------|
|      |               |           |              |                |            |        |
|      |               |           |              |                |            |        |
|      |               |           |              |                |            |        |
|      |               |           |              |                |            |        |
|      |               |           |              |                |            |        |
|      |               |           |              |                |            |        |
|      |               |           |              |                |            |        |
|      |               |           |              |                |            |        |
|      |               |           |              |                |            |        |
|      |               |           |              |                |            |        |
|      |               |           |              |                |            |        |
|      |               |           |              |                |            |        |
|      |               |           |              |                |            |        |
|      |               |           |              |                |            |        |
|      |               |           |              |                |            |        |
|      |               |           |              |                |            |        |
|      |               |           |              |                |            |        |
|      |               |           |              |                |            |        |
|      |               |           |              |                |            |        |
|      |               |           |              |                |            |        |
|      |               |           |              |                |            |        |
|      |               |           |              |                |            |        |
|      |               |           |              |                |            |        |
|      |               |           |              |                |            |        |
|      |               |           |              |                |            |        |
|      |               |           |              |                |            |        |
|      |               |           |              |                |            |        |
|      |               |           |              |                |            |        |

Total

# Purchase & Sales Tracker

DATES FROM _____

| Item | Purchase Date | Sale Date | Sale Website | Purchase Price | Sale Price | Profit |
|------|---------------|-----------|--------------|----------------|------------|--------|
|      |               |           |              |                |            |        |
|      |               |           |              |                |            |        |
|      |               |           |              |                |            |        |
|      |               |           |              |                |            |        |
|      |               |           |              |                |            |        |
|      |               |           |              |                |            |        |
|      |               |           |              |                |            |        |
|      |               |           |              |                |            |        |
|      |               |           |              |                |            |        |
|      |               |           |              |                |            |        |
|      |               |           |              |                |            |        |
|      |               |           |              |                |            |        |
|      |               |           |              |                |            |        |
|      |               |           |              |                |            |        |
|      |               |           |              |                |            |        |
|      |               |           |              |                |            |        |
|      |               |           |              |                |            |        |
|      |               |           |              |                |            |        |
|      |               |           |              |                |            |        |
|      |               |           |              |                |            |        |
|      |               |           |              |                |            |        |
|      |               |           |              |                |            |        |
|      |               |           |              |                |            |        |
|      |               |           |              |                |            |        |
|      |               |           |              |                |            |        |
|      |               |           |              |                |            |        |
|      |               |           |              |                |            |        |

Total

# Purchase & Sales Tracker

DATES FROM _____

| Item | Purchase Date | Sale Date | Sale Website | Purchase Price | Sale Price | Profit |
|------|---------------|-----------|--------------|----------------|------------|--------|
|  |  |  |  |  |  |  |
|  |  |  |  |  |  |  |
|  |  |  |  |  |  |  |
|  |  |  |  |  |  |  |
|  |  |  |  |  |  |  |
|  |  |  |  |  |  |  |
|  |  |  |  |  |  |  |
|  |  |  |  |  |  |  |
|  |  |  |  |  |  |  |
|  |  |  |  |  |  |  |
|  |  |  |  |  |  |  |
|  |  |  |  |  |  |  |
|  |  |  |  |  |  |  |
|  |  |  |  |  |  |  |
|  |  |  |  |  |  |  |
|  |  |  |  |  |  |  |
|  |  |  |  |  |  |  |
|  |  |  |  |  |  |  |
|  |  |  |  |  |  |  |
|  |  |  |  |  |  |  |
|  |  |  |  |  |  |  |
|  |  |  |  |  |  |  |
|  |  |  |  |  |  |  |
|  |  |  |  |  |  |  |
|  |  |  |  |  |  |  |
|  |  |  |  |  |  |  |
|  |  |  |  |  |  |  |

Total

# Purchase & Sales Tracker

DATES FROM _____

| Item | Purchase Date | Sale Date | Sale Website | Purchase Price | Sale Price | Profit |
|------|---------------|-----------|--------------|----------------|------------|--------|
|  |  |  |  |  |  |  |
|  |  |  |  |  |  |  |
|  |  |  |  |  |  |  |
|  |  |  |  |  |  |  |
|  |  |  |  |  |  |  |
|  |  |  |  |  |  |  |
|  |  |  |  |  |  |  |
|  |  |  |  |  |  |  |
|  |  |  |  |  |  |  |
|  |  |  |  |  |  |  |
|  |  |  |  |  |  |  |
|  |  |  |  |  |  |  |
|  |  |  |  |  |  |  |
|  |  |  |  |  |  |  |
|  |  |  |  |  |  |  |
|  |  |  |  |  |  |  |
|  |  |  |  |  |  |  |
|  |  |  |  |  |  |  |
|  |  |  |  |  |  |  |
|  |  |  |  |  |  |  |
|  |  |  |  |  |  |  |
|  |  |  |  |  |  |  |
|  |  |  |  |  |  |  |
|  |  |  |  |  |  |  |
|  |  |  |  |  |  |  |
|  |  |  |  |  |  |  |
|  |  |  |  |  |  |  |

Total

# Purchase & Sales Tracker

DATES FROM _____

| Item | Purchase Date | Sale Date | Sale Website | Purchase Price | Sale Price | Profit |
|------|---------------|-----------|--------------|----------------|------------|--------|
|      |               |           |              |                |            |        |
|      |               |           |              |                |            |        |
|      |               |           |              |                |            |        |
|      |               |           |              |                |            |        |
|      |               |           |              |                |            |        |
|      |               |           |              |                |            |        |
|      |               |           |              |                |            |        |
|      |               |           |              |                |            |        |
|      |               |           |              |                |            |        |
|      |               |           |              |                |            |        |
|      |               |           |              |                |            |        |
|      |               |           |              |                |            |        |
|      |               |           |              |                |            |        |
|      |               |           |              |                |            |        |
|      |               |           |              |                |            |        |
|      |               |           |              |                |            |        |
|      |               |           |              |                |            |        |
|      |               |           |              |                |            |        |
|      |               |           |              |                |            |        |
|      |               |           |              |                |            |        |
|      |               |           |              |                |            |        |
|      |               |           |              |                |            |        |
|      |               |           |              |                |            |        |
|      |               |           |              |                |            |        |
|      |               |           |              |                |            |        |
|      |               |           |              |                |            |        |
|      |               |           |              |                |            |        |

Total

# Purchase & Sales Tracker

DATES FROM _____

| Item | Purchase Date | Sale Date | Sale Website | Purchase Price | Sale Price | Profit |
|------|---------------|-----------|--------------|----------------|------------|--------|
|  |  |  |  |  |  |  |
|  |  |  |  |  |  |  |
|  |  |  |  |  |  |  |
|  |  |  |  |  |  |  |
|  |  |  |  |  |  |  |
|  |  |  |  |  |  |  |
|  |  |  |  |  |  |  |
|  |  |  |  |  |  |  |
|  |  |  |  |  |  |  |
|  |  |  |  |  |  |  |
|  |  |  |  |  |  |  |
|  |  |  |  |  |  |  |
|  |  |  |  |  |  |  |
|  |  |  |  |  |  |  |
|  |  |  |  |  |  |  |
|  |  |  |  |  |  |  |
|  |  |  |  |  |  |  |
|  |  |  |  |  |  |  |
|  |  |  |  |  |  |  |
|  |  |  |  |  |  |  |
|  |  |  |  |  |  |  |
|  |  |  |  |  |  |  |
|  |  |  |  |  |  |  |
|  |  |  |  |  |  |  |
|  |  |  |  |  |  |  |
|  |  |  |  |  |  |  |
|  |  |  |  |  |  |  |
|  |  |  |  |  |  |  |
|  |  |  |  |  |  |  |

Total

# Purchase & Sales Tracker

DATES FROM _____

| Item | Purchase Date | Sale Date | Sale Website | Purchase Price | Sale Price | Profit |
|------|---------------|-----------|--------------|----------------|------------|--------|
|      |               |           |              |                |            |        |
|      |               |           |              |                |            |        |
|      |               |           |              |                |            |        |
|      |               |           |              |                |            |        |
|      |               |           |              |                |            |        |
|      |               |           |              |                |            |        |
|      |               |           |              |                |            |        |
|      |               |           |              |                |            |        |
|      |               |           |              |                |            |        |
|      |               |           |              |                |            |        |
|      |               |           |              |                |            |        |
|      |               |           |              |                |            |        |
|      |               |           |              |                |            |        |
|      |               |           |              |                |            |        |
|      |               |           |              |                |            |        |
|      |               |           |              |                |            |        |
|      |               |           |              |                |            |        |
|      |               |           |              |                |            |        |
|      |               |           |              |                |            |        |
|      |               |           |              |                |            |        |
|      |               |           |              |                |            |        |
|      |               |           |              |                |            |        |
|      |               |           |              |                |            |        |
|      |               |           |              |                |            |        |
|      |               |           |              |                |            |        |
|      |               |           |              |                |            |        |
|      |               |           |              |                |            |        |
|      |               |           |              |                |            |        |

Total

# Purchase & Sales Tracker

DATES FROM _____

| Item | Purchase Date | Sale Date | Sale Website | Purchase Price | Sale Price | Profit |
|------|---------------|-----------|--------------|----------------|------------|--------|
|  |  |  |  |  |  |  |
|  |  |  |  |  |  |  |
|  |  |  |  |  |  |  |
|  |  |  |  |  |  |  |
|  |  |  |  |  |  |  |
|  |  |  |  |  |  |  |
|  |  |  |  |  |  |  |
|  |  |  |  |  |  |  |
|  |  |  |  |  |  |  |
|  |  |  |  |  |  |  |
|  |  |  |  |  |  |  |
|  |  |  |  |  |  |  |
|  |  |  |  |  |  |  |
|  |  |  |  |  |  |  |
|  |  |  |  |  |  |  |
|  |  |  |  |  |  |  |
|  |  |  |  |  |  |  |
|  |  |  |  |  |  |  |
|  |  |  |  |  |  |  |
|  |  |  |  |  |  |  |
|  |  |  |  |  |  |  |
|  |  |  |  |  |  |  |
|  |  |  |  |  |  |  |
|  |  |  |  |  |  |  |
|  |  |  |  |  |  |  |
|  |  |  |  |  |  |  |

Total

# Purchase & Sales Tracker

DATES FROM _____

| Item | Purchase Date | Sale Date | Sale Website | Purchase Price | Sale Price | Profit |
|------|---------------|-----------|--------------|----------------|------------|--------|
|  |  |  |  |  |  |  |
|  |  |  |  |  |  |  |
|  |  |  |  |  |  |  |
|  |  |  |  |  |  |  |
|  |  |  |  |  |  |  |
|  |  |  |  |  |  |  |
|  |  |  |  |  |  |  |
|  |  |  |  |  |  |  |
|  |  |  |  |  |  |  |
|  |  |  |  |  |  |  |
|  |  |  |  |  |  |  |
|  |  |  |  |  |  |  |
|  |  |  |  |  |  |  |
|  |  |  |  |  |  |  |
|  |  |  |  |  |  |  |
|  |  |  |  |  |  |  |
|  |  |  |  |  |  |  |
|  |  |  |  |  |  |  |
|  |  |  |  |  |  |  |
|  |  |  |  |  |  |  |
|  |  |  |  |  |  |  |
|  |  |  |  |  |  |  |
|  |  |  |  |  |  |  |
|  |  |  |  |  |  |  |
|  |  |  |  |  |  |  |
|  |  |  |  |  |  |  |
|  |  |  |  |  |  |  |
|  |  |  |  |  |  |  |

Total

# Purchase & Sales Tracker

DATES FROM _____

| Item | Purchase Date | Sale Date | Sale Website | Purchase Price | Sale Price | Profit |
|------|--------------|-----------|--------------|----------------|------------|--------|
|  |  |  |  |  |  |  |
|  |  |  |  |  |  |  |
|  |  |  |  |  |  |  |
|  |  |  |  |  |  |  |
|  |  |  |  |  |  |  |
|  |  |  |  |  |  |  |
|  |  |  |  |  |  |  |
|  |  |  |  |  |  |  |
|  |  |  |  |  |  |  |
|  |  |  |  |  |  |  |
|  |  |  |  |  |  |  |
|  |  |  |  |  |  |  |
|  |  |  |  |  |  |  |
|  |  |  |  |  |  |  |
|  |  |  |  |  |  |  |
|  |  |  |  |  |  |  |
|  |  |  |  |  |  |  |
|  |  |  |  |  |  |  |
|  |  |  |  |  |  |  |
|  |  |  |  |  |  |  |
|  |  |  |  |  |  |  |
|  |  |  |  |  |  |  |
|  |  |  |  |  |  |  |
|  |  |  |  |  |  |  |
|  |  |  |  |  |  |  |
|  |  |  |  |  |  |  |

Total

# Purchase & Sales Tracker

DATES FROM _____

| Item | Purchase Date | Sale Date | Sale Website | Purchase Price | Sale Price | Profit |
|---|---|---|---|---|---|---|
|  |  |  |  |  |  |  |
|  |  |  |  |  |  |  |
|  |  |  |  |  |  |  |
|  |  |  |  |  |  |  |
|  |  |  |  |  |  |  |
|  |  |  |  |  |  |  |
|  |  |  |  |  |  |  |
|  |  |  |  |  |  |  |
|  |  |  |  |  |  |  |
|  |  |  |  |  |  |  |
|  |  |  |  |  |  |  |
|  |  |  |  |  |  |  |
|  |  |  |  |  |  |  |
|  |  |  |  |  |  |  |
|  |  |  |  |  |  |  |
|  |  |  |  |  |  |  |
|  |  |  |  |  |  |  |
|  |  |  |  |  |  |  |
|  |  |  |  |  |  |  |
|  |  |  |  |  |  |  |
|  |  |  |  |  |  |  |
|  |  |  |  |  |  |  |
|  |  |  |  |  |  |  |
|  |  |  |  |  |  |  |
|  |  |  |  |  |  |  |
|  |  |  |  |  |  |  |
|  |  |  |  |  |  |  |

Total

# Purchase & Sales Tracker

DATES FROM _____

| Item | Purchase Date | Sale Date | Sale Website | Purchase Price | Sale Price | Profit |
|------|---------------|-----------|--------------|----------------|------------|--------|
|      |               |           |              |                |            |        |
|      |               |           |              |                |            |        |
|      |               |           |              |                |            |        |
|      |               |           |              |                |            |        |
|      |               |           |              |                |            |        |
|      |               |           |              |                |            |        |
|      |               |           |              |                |            |        |
|      |               |           |              |                |            |        |
|      |               |           |              |                |            |        |
|      |               |           |              |                |            |        |
|      |               |           |              |                |            |        |
|      |               |           |              |                |            |        |
|      |               |           |              |                |            |        |
|      |               |           |              |                |            |        |
|      |               |           |              |                |            |        |
|      |               |           |              |                |            |        |
|      |               |           |              |                |            |        |
|      |               |           |              |                |            |        |
|      |               |           |              |                |            |        |
|      |               |           |              |                |            |        |
|      |               |           |              |                |            |        |
|      |               |           |              |                |            |        |
|      |               |           |              |                |            |        |
|      |               |           |              |                |            |        |
|      |               |           |              |                |            |        |
|      |               |           |              |                |            |        |
|      |               |           |              |                |            |        |
|      |               |           |              |                |            |        |
|      |               |           |              |                |            |        |

Total

# Purchase & Sales Tracker

| Item | Purchase Date | Sale Date | Sale Website | Purchase Price | Sale Price | Profit |
|------|---------------|-----------|--------------|----------------|------------|--------|
|      |               |           |              |                |            |        |
|      |               |           |              |                |            |        |
|      |               |           |              |                |            |        |
|      |               |           |              |                |            |        |
|      |               |           |              |                |            |        |
|      |               |           |              |                |            |        |
|      |               |           |              |                |            |        |
|      |               |           |              |                |            |        |
|      |               |           |              |                |            |        |
|      |               |           |              |                |            |        |
|      |               |           |              |                |            |        |
|      |               |           |              |                |            |        |
|      |               |           |              |                |            |        |
|      |               |           |              |                |            |        |
|      |               |           |              |                |            |        |
|      |               |           |              |                |            |        |
|      |               |           |              |                |            |        |
|      |               |           |              |                |            |        |
|      |               |           |              |                |            |        |
|      |               |           |              |                |            |        |
|      |               |           |              |                |            |        |
|      |               |           |              |                |            |        |
|      |               |           |              |                |            |        |
|      |               |           |              |                |            |        |
|      |               |           |              |                |            |        |
|      |               |           |              |                |            |        |
|      |               |           |              |                |            |        |

Total

# Purchase & Sales Tracker

DATES FROM _____

| Item | Purchase Date | Sale Date | Sale Website | Purchase Price | Sale Price | Profit |
|------|---------------|-----------|--------------|----------------|------------|--------|
|  |  |  |  |  |  |  |
|  |  |  |  |  |  |  |
|  |  |  |  |  |  |  |
|  |  |  |  |  |  |  |
|  |  |  |  |  |  |  |
|  |  |  |  |  |  |  |
|  |  |  |  |  |  |  |
|  |  |  |  |  |  |  |
|  |  |  |  |  |  |  |
|  |  |  |  |  |  |  |
|  |  |  |  |  |  |  |
|  |  |  |  |  |  |  |
|  |  |  |  |  |  |  |
|  |  |  |  |  |  |  |
|  |  |  |  |  |  |  |
|  |  |  |  |  |  |  |
|  |  |  |  |  |  |  |
|  |  |  |  |  |  |  |
|  |  |  |  |  |  |  |
|  |  |  |  |  |  |  |
|  |  |  |  |  |  |  |
|  |  |  |  |  |  |  |
|  |  |  |  |  |  |  |
|  |  |  |  |  |  |  |
|  |  |  |  |  |  |  |
|  |  |  |  |  |  |  |

Total

# Purchase & Sales Tracker

DATES FROM _____

| Item | Purchase Date | Sale Date | Sale Website | Purchase Price | Sale Price | Profit |
|------|---------------|-----------|--------------|----------------|------------|--------|
|      |               |           |              |                |            |        |
|      |               |           |              |                |            |        |
|      |               |           |              |                |            |        |
|      |               |           |              |                |            |        |
|      |               |           |              |                |            |        |
|      |               |           |              |                |            |        |
|      |               |           |              |                |            |        |
|      |               |           |              |                |            |        |
|      |               |           |              |                |            |        |
|      |               |           |              |                |            |        |
|      |               |           |              |                |            |        |
|      |               |           |              |                |            |        |
|      |               |           |              |                |            |        |
|      |               |           |              |                |            |        |
|      |               |           |              |                |            |        |
|      |               |           |              |                |            |        |
|      |               |           |              |                |            |        |
|      |               |           |              |                |            |        |
|      |               |           |              |                |            |        |
|      |               |           |              |                |            |        |
|      |               |           |              |                |            |        |
|      |               |           |              |                |            |        |
|      |               |           |              |                |            |        |
|      |               |           |              |                |            |        |
|      |               |           |              |                |            |        |
|      |               |           |              |                |            |        |
|      |               |           |              |                |            |        |
|      |               |           |              |                |            |        |

Total

# Purchase & Sales Tracker

| Item | Purchase Date | Sale Date | Sale Website | Purchase Price | Sale Price | Profit |
|------|---------------|-----------|--------------|----------------|------------|--------|
|  |  |  |  |  |  |  |
|  |  |  |  |  |  |  |
|  |  |  |  |  |  |  |
|  |  |  |  |  |  |  |
|  |  |  |  |  |  |  |
|  |  |  |  |  |  |  |
|  |  |  |  |  |  |  |
|  |  |  |  |  |  |  |
|  |  |  |  |  |  |  |
|  |  |  |  |  |  |  |
|  |  |  |  |  |  |  |
|  |  |  |  |  |  |  |
|  |  |  |  |  |  |  |
|  |  |  |  |  |  |  |
|  |  |  |  |  |  |  |
|  |  |  |  |  |  |  |
|  |  |  |  |  |  |  |
|  |  |  |  |  |  |  |
|  |  |  |  |  |  |  |
|  |  |  |  |  |  |  |
|  |  |  |  |  |  |  |
|  |  |  |  |  |  |  |
|  |  |  |  |  |  |  |
|  |  |  |  |  |  |  |
|  |  |  |  |  |  |  |
|  |  |  |  |  |  |  |

**Total**

# Purchase & Sales Tracker

DATES FROM _____

| Item | Purchase Date | Sale Date | Sale Website | Purchase Price | Sale Price | Profit |
|------|---------------|-----------|--------------|----------------|------------|--------|
| | | | | | | |
| | | | | | | |
| | | | | | | |
| | | | | | | |
| | | | | | | |
| | | | | | | |
| | | | | | | |
| | | | | | | |
| | | | | | | |
| | | | | | | |
| | | | | | | |
| | | | | | | |
| | | | | | | |
| | | | | | | |
| | | | | | | |
| | | | | | | |
| | | | | | | |
| | | | | | | |
| | | | | | | |
| | | | | | | |
| | | | | | | |
| | | | | | | |
| | | | | | | |
| | | | | | | |
| | | | | | | |
| | | | | | | |

**Total**

# Purchase & Sales Tracker

DATES FROM _____

| Item | Purchase Date | Sale Date | Sale Website | Purchase Price | Sale Price | Profit |
|---|---|---|---|---|---|---|
| | | | | | | |
| | | | | | | |
| | | | | | | |
| | | | | | | |
| | | | | | | |
| | | | | | | |
| | | | | | | |
| | | | | | | |
| | | | | | | |
| | | | | | | |
| | | | | | | |
| | | | | | | |
| | | | | | | |
| | | | | | | |
| | | | | | | |
| | | | | | | |
| | | | | | | |
| | | | | | | |
| | | | | | | |
| | | | | | | |
| | | | | | | |
| | | | | | | |
| | | | | | | |
| | | | | | | |

**Total** | | | |

# Purchase & Sales Tracker

DATES FROM _____

| Item | Purchase Date | Sale Date | Sale Website | Purchase Price | Sale Price | Profit |
|------|---------------|-----------|--------------|----------------|------------|--------|
|  |  |  |  |  |  |  |
|  |  |  |  |  |  |  |
|  |  |  |  |  |  |  |
|  |  |  |  |  |  |  |
|  |  |  |  |  |  |  |
|  |  |  |  |  |  |  |
|  |  |  |  |  |  |  |
|  |  |  |  |  |  |  |
|  |  |  |  |  |  |  |
|  |  |  |  |  |  |  |
|  |  |  |  |  |  |  |
|  |  |  |  |  |  |  |
|  |  |  |  |  |  |  |
|  |  |  |  |  |  |  |
|  |  |  |  |  |  |  |
|  |  |  |  |  |  |  |
|  |  |  |  |  |  |  |
|  |  |  |  |  |  |  |
|  |  |  |  |  |  |  |
|  |  |  |  |  |  |  |
|  |  |  |  |  |  |  |
|  |  |  |  |  |  |  |
|  |  |  |  |  |  |  |
|  |  |  |  |  |  |  |
|  |  |  |  |  |  |  |
|  |  |  |  |  |  |  |
|  |  |  |  |  |  |  |
|  |  |  |  |  |  |  |
|  |  |  |  |  |  |  |

Total _____ _____ _____

# Purchase & Sales Tracker

DATES FROM _____

| Item | Purchase Date | Sale Date | Sale Website | Purchase Price | Sale Price | Profit |
|------|---------------|-----------|--------------|----------------|------------|--------|
|      |               |           |              |                |            |        |
|      |               |           |              |                |            |        |
|      |               |           |              |                |            |        |
|      |               |           |              |                |            |        |
|      |               |           |              |                |            |        |
|      |               |           |              |                |            |        |
|      |               |           |              |                |            |        |
|      |               |           |              |                |            |        |
|      |               |           |              |                |            |        |
|      |               |           |              |                |            |        |
|      |               |           |              |                |            |        |
|      |               |           |              |                |            |        |
|      |               |           |              |                |            |        |
|      |               |           |              |                |            |        |
|      |               |           |              |                |            |        |
|      |               |           |              |                |            |        |
|      |               |           |              |                |            |        |
|      |               |           |              |                |            |        |
|      |               |           |              |                |            |        |
|      |               |           |              |                |            |        |
|      |               |           |              |                |            |        |
|      |               |           |              |                |            |        |
|      |               |           |              |                |            |        |
|      |               |           |              |                |            |        |
|      |               |           |              |                |            |        |
|      |               |           |              |                |            |        |
|      |               |           |              |                |            |        |

Total

# Purchase & Sales Tracker

DATES FROM _____

| Item | Purchase Date | Sale Date | Sale Website | Purchase Price | Sale Price | Profit |
|------|------|------|------|------|------|------|
| | | | | | | |
| | | | | | | |
| | | | | | | |
| | | | | | | |
| | | | | | | |
| | | | | | | |
| | | | | | | |
| | | | | | | |
| | | | | | | |
| | | | | | | |
| | | | | | | |
| | | | | | | |
| | | | | | | |
| | | | | | | |
| | | | | | | |
| | | | | | | |
| | | | | | | |
| | | | | | | |
| | | | | | | |
| | | | | | | |
| | | | | | | |
| | | | | | | |
| | | | | | | |
| | | | | | | |
| | | | | | | |
| | | | | | | |

Total

# Purchase & Sales Tracker

DATES FROM _____

| Item | Purchase Date | Sale Date | Sale Website | Purchase Price | Sale Price | Profit |
|---|---|---|---|---|---|---|
| | | | | | | |
| | | | | | | |
| | | | | | | |
| | | | | | | |
| | | | | | | |
| | | | | | | |
| | | | | | | |
| | | | | | | |
| | | | | | | |
| | | | | | | |
| | | | | | | |
| | | | | | | |
| | | | | | | |
| | | | | | | |
| | | | | | | |
| | | | | | | |
| | | | | | | |
| | | | | | | |
| | | | | | | |
| | | | | | | |
| | | | | | | |
| | | | | | | |
| | | | | | | |
| | | | | | | |
| | | | | | | |
| | | | | | | |
| | | | | | | |
| | | | | | | |
| | | | | | | |
| | | | | | | |
| | | | | | | |

**Total**

# Purchase & Sales Tracker

DATES FROM _____

| Item | Purchase Date | Sale Date | Sale Website | Purchase Price | Sale Price | Profit |
|------|---------------|-----------|--------------|----------------|------------|--------|
|  |  |  |  |  |  |  |
|  |  |  |  |  |  |  |
|  |  |  |  |  |  |  |
|  |  |  |  |  |  |  |
|  |  |  |  |  |  |  |
|  |  |  |  |  |  |  |
|  |  |  |  |  |  |  |
|  |  |  |  |  |  |  |
|  |  |  |  |  |  |  |
|  |  |  |  |  |  |  |
|  |  |  |  |  |  |  |
|  |  |  |  |  |  |  |
|  |  |  |  |  |  |  |
|  |  |  |  |  |  |  |
|  |  |  |  |  |  |  |
|  |  |  |  |  |  |  |
|  |  |  |  |  |  |  |
|  |  |  |  |  |  |  |
|  |  |  |  |  |  |  |
|  |  |  |  |  |  |  |
|  |  |  |  |  |  |  |
|  |  |  |  |  |  |  |
|  |  |  |  |  |  |  |
|  |  |  |  |  |  |  |
|  |  |  |  |  |  |  |
|  |  |  |  |  |  |  |
|  |  |  |  |  |  |  |

Total

# Purchase & Sales Tracker

DATES FROM _____

| Item | Purchase Date | Sale Date | Sale Website | Purchase Price | Sale Price | Profit |
|---|---|---|---|---|---|---|
| | | | | | | |
| | | | | | | |
| | | | | | | |
| | | | | | | |
| | | | | | | |
| | | | | | | |
| | | | | | | |
| | | | | | | |
| | | | | | | |
| | | | | | | |
| | | | | | | |
| | | | | | | |
| | | | | | | |
| | | | | | | |
| | | | | | | |
| | | | | | | |
| | | | | | | |
| | | | | | | |
| | | | | | | |
| | | | | | | |
| | | | | | | |
| | | | | | | |
| | | | | | | |
| | | | | | | |
| | | | | | | |
| | | | | | | |
| | | | | | | |

Total

# Purchase & Sales Tracker

DATES FROM _____

| Item | Purchase Date | Sale Date | Sale Website | Purchase Price | Sale Price | Profit |
|------|--------------|-----------|--------------|----------------|------------|--------|
|  |  |  |  |  |  |  |
|  |  |  |  |  |  |  |
|  |  |  |  |  |  |  |
|  |  |  |  |  |  |  |
|  |  |  |  |  |  |  |
|  |  |  |  |  |  |  |
|  |  |  |  |  |  |  |
|  |  |  |  |  |  |  |
|  |  |  |  |  |  |  |
|  |  |  |  |  |  |  |
|  |  |  |  |  |  |  |
|  |  |  |  |  |  |  |
|  |  |  |  |  |  |  |
|  |  |  |  |  |  |  |
|  |  |  |  |  |  |  |
|  |  |  |  |  |  |  |
|  |  |  |  |  |  |  |
|  |  |  |  |  |  |  |
|  |  |  |  |  |  |  |
|  |  |  |  |  |  |  |
|  |  |  |  |  |  |  |
|  |  |  |  |  |  |  |
|  |  |  |  |  |  |  |
|  |  |  |  |  |  |  |
|  |  |  |  |  |  |  |
|  |  |  |  |  |  |  |
|  |  |  |  |  |  |  |
|  |  |  |  |  |  |  |

Total

# Purchase & Sales Tracker

DATES FROM _____

| Item | Purchase Date | Sale Date | Sale Website | Purchase Price | Sale Price | Profit |
|---|---|---|---|---|---|---|
| | | | | | | |
| | | | | | | |
| | | | | | | |
| | | | | | | |
| | | | | | | |
| | | | | | | |
| | | | | | | |
| | | | | | | |
| | | | | | | |
| | | | | | | |
| | | | | | | |
| | | | | | | |
| | | | | | | |
| | | | | | | |
| | | | | | | |
| | | | | | | |
| | | | | | | |
| | | | | | | |
| | | | | | | |
| | | | | | | |
| | | | | | | |
| | | | | | | |
| | | | | | | |
| | | | | | | |
| | | | | | | |
| | | | | | | |

Total

# Purchase & Sales Tracker

DATES FROM _____

| Item | Purchase Date | Sale Date | Sale Website | Purchase Price | Sale Price | Profit |
|------|--------------|-----------|--------------|----------------|------------|--------|
|  |  |  |  |  |  |  |
|  |  |  |  |  |  |  |
|  |  |  |  |  |  |  |
|  |  |  |  |  |  |  |
|  |  |  |  |  |  |  |
|  |  |  |  |  |  |  |
|  |  |  |  |  |  |  |
|  |  |  |  |  |  |  |
|  |  |  |  |  |  |  |
|  |  |  |  |  |  |  |
|  |  |  |  |  |  |  |
|  |  |  |  |  |  |  |
|  |  |  |  |  |  |  |
|  |  |  |  |  |  |  |
|  |  |  |  |  |  |  |
|  |  |  |  |  |  |  |
|  |  |  |  |  |  |  |
|  |  |  |  |  |  |  |
|  |  |  |  |  |  |  |
|  |  |  |  |  |  |  |
|  |  |  |  |  |  |  |
|  |  |  |  |  |  |  |
|  |  |  |  |  |  |  |
|  |  |  |  |  |  |  |
|  |  |  |  |  |  |  |
|  |  |  |  |  |  |  |
|  |  |  |  |  |  |  |
|  |  |  |  |  |  |  |

Total

# Purchase & Sales Tracker

DATES FROM _____

| Item | Purchase Date | Sale Date | Sale Website | Purchase Price | Sale Price | Profit |
|------|---------------|-----------|--------------|----------------|------------|--------|
|  |  |  |  |  |  |  |
|  |  |  |  |  |  |  |
|  |  |  |  |  |  |  |
|  |  |  |  |  |  |  |
|  |  |  |  |  |  |  |
|  |  |  |  |  |  |  |
|  |  |  |  |  |  |  |
|  |  |  |  |  |  |  |
|  |  |  |  |  |  |  |
|  |  |  |  |  |  |  |
|  |  |  |  |  |  |  |
|  |  |  |  |  |  |  |
|  |  |  |  |  |  |  |
|  |  |  |  |  |  |  |
|  |  |  |  |  |  |  |
|  |  |  |  |  |  |  |
|  |  |  |  |  |  |  |
|  |  |  |  |  |  |  |
|  |  |  |  |  |  |  |
|  |  |  |  |  |  |  |
|  |  |  |  |  |  |  |
|  |  |  |  |  |  |  |
|  |  |  |  |  |  |  |
|  |  |  |  |  |  |  |
|  |  |  |  |  |  |  |
|  |  |  |  |  |  |  |
|  |  |  |  |  |  |  |
|  |  |  |  |  |  |  |

Total

# Purchase & Sales Tracker

DATES FROM _____

| Item | Purchase Date | Sale Date | Sale Website | Purchase Price | Sale Price | Profit |
|------|---------------|-----------|--------------|----------------|------------|--------|
|      |               |           |              |                |            |        |
|      |               |           |              |                |            |        |
|      |               |           |              |                |            |        |
|      |               |           |              |                |            |        |
|      |               |           |              |                |            |        |
|      |               |           |              |                |            |        |
|      |               |           |              |                |            |        |
|      |               |           |              |                |            |        |
|      |               |           |              |                |            |        |
|      |               |           |              |                |            |        |
|      |               |           |              |                |            |        |
|      |               |           |              |                |            |        |
|      |               |           |              |                |            |        |
|      |               |           |              |                |            |        |
|      |               |           |              |                |            |        |
|      |               |           |              |                |            |        |
|      |               |           |              |                |            |        |
|      |               |           |              |                |            |        |
|      |               |           |              |                |            |        |
|      |               |           |              |                |            |        |
|      |               |           |              |                |            |        |
|      |               |           |              |                |            |        |
|      |               |           |              |                |            |        |
|      |               |           |              |                |            |        |
|      |               |           |              |                |            |        |
|      |               |           |              |                |            |        |
|      |               |           |              |                |            |        |
|      |               |           |              |                |            |        |

Total

# Purchase & Sales Tracker

DATES FROM _____

| Item | Purchase Date | Sale Date | Sale Website | Purchase Price | Sale Price | Profit |
|------|---------------|-----------|--------------|----------------|------------|--------|
|  |  |  |  |  |  |  |
|  |  |  |  |  |  |  |
|  |  |  |  |  |  |  |
|  |  |  |  |  |  |  |
|  |  |  |  |  |  |  |
|  |  |  |  |  |  |  |
|  |  |  |  |  |  |  |
|  |  |  |  |  |  |  |
|  |  |  |  |  |  |  |
|  |  |  |  |  |  |  |
|  |  |  |  |  |  |  |
|  |  |  |  |  |  |  |
|  |  |  |  |  |  |  |
|  |  |  |  |  |  |  |
|  |  |  |  |  |  |  |
|  |  |  |  |  |  |  |
|  |  |  |  |  |  |  |
|  |  |  |  |  |  |  |
|  |  |  |  |  |  |  |
|  |  |  |  |  |  |  |
|  |  |  |  |  |  |  |
|  |  |  |  |  |  |  |
|  |  |  |  |  |  |  |
|  |  |  |  |  |  |  |
|  |  |  |  |  |  |  |
|  |  |  |  |  |  |  |
|  |  |  |  |  |  |  |

Total

# Purchase & Sales Tracker

DATES FROM _____

| Item | Purchase Date | Sale Date | Sale Website | Purchase Price | Sale Price | Profit |
|------|---------------|-----------|--------------|----------------|------------|--------|
|      |               |           |              |                |            |        |
|      |               |           |              |                |            |        |
|      |               |           |              |                |            |        |
|      |               |           |              |                |            |        |
|      |               |           |              |                |            |        |
|      |               |           |              |                |            |        |
|      |               |           |              |                |            |        |
|      |               |           |              |                |            |        |
|      |               |           |              |                |            |        |
|      |               |           |              |                |            |        |
|      |               |           |              |                |            |        |
|      |               |           |              |                |            |        |
|      |               |           |              |                |            |        |
|      |               |           |              |                |            |        |
|      |               |           |              |                |            |        |
|      |               |           |              |                |            |        |
|      |               |           |              |                |            |        |
|      |               |           |              |                |            |        |
|      |               |           |              |                |            |        |
|      |               |           |              |                |            |        |
|      |               |           |              |                |            |        |
|      |               |           |              |                |            |        |
|      |               |           |              |                |            |        |
|      |               |           |              |                |            |        |
|      |               |           |              |                |            |        |
|      |               |           |              |                |            |        |
|      |               |           |              |                |            |        |

Total

# Purchase & Sales Tracker

DATES FROM _____

| Item | Purchase Date | Sale Date | Sale Website | Purchase Price | Sale Price | Profit |
|---|---|---|---|---|---|---|
| | | | | | | |
| | | | | | | |
| | | | | | | |
| | | | | | | |
| | | | | | | |
| | | | | | | |
| | | | | | | |
| | | | | | | |
| | | | | | | |
| | | | | | | |
| | | | | | | |
| | | | | | | |
| | | | | | | |
| | | | | | | |
| | | | | | | |
| | | | | | | |
| | | | | | | |
| | | | | | | |
| | | | | | | |
| | | | | | | |
| | | | | | | |
| | | | | | | |
| | | | | | | |
| | | | | | | |
| | | | | | | |
| | | | | | | |
| | | | | | | |

Total

# Purchase & Sales Tracker

| Item | Purchase Date | Sale Date | Sale Website | Purchase Price | Sale Price | Profit |
|------|---------------|-----------|--------------|----------------|------------|--------|
|      |               |           |              |                |            |        |
|      |               |           |              |                |            |        |
|      |               |           |              |                |            |        |
|      |               |           |              |                |            |        |
|      |               |           |              |                |            |        |
|      |               |           |              |                |            |        |
|      |               |           |              |                |            |        |
|      |               |           |              |                |            |        |
|      |               |           |              |                |            |        |
|      |               |           |              |                |            |        |
|      |               |           |              |                |            |        |
|      |               |           |              |                |            |        |
|      |               |           |              |                |            |        |
|      |               |           |              |                |            |        |
|      |               |           |              |                |            |        |
|      |               |           |              |                |            |        |
|      |               |           |              |                |            |        |
|      |               |           |              |                |            |        |
|      |               |           |              |                |            |        |
|      |               |           |              |                |            |        |
|      |               |           |              |                |            |        |
|      |               |           |              |                |            |        |
|      |               |           |              |                |            |        |
|      |               |           |              |                |            |        |
|      |               |           |              |                |            |        |
|      |               |           |              |                |            |        |
|      |               |           |              |                |            |        |
|      |               |           |              |                |            |        |
|      |               |           |              |                |            |        |

Total

# Purchase & Sales Tracker

DATES FROM _____

| Item | Purchase Date | Sale Date | Sale Website | Purchase Price | Sale Price | Profit |
|------|---------------|-----------|--------------|----------------|------------|--------|
|  |  |  |  |  |  |  |
|  |  |  |  |  |  |  |
|  |  |  |  |  |  |  |
|  |  |  |  |  |  |  |
|  |  |  |  |  |  |  |
|  |  |  |  |  |  |  |
|  |  |  |  |  |  |  |
|  |  |  |  |  |  |  |
|  |  |  |  |  |  |  |
|  |  |  |  |  |  |  |
|  |  |  |  |  |  |  |
|  |  |  |  |  |  |  |
|  |  |  |  |  |  |  |
|  |  |  |  |  |  |  |
|  |  |  |  |  |  |  |
|  |  |  |  |  |  |  |
|  |  |  |  |  |  |  |
|  |  |  |  |  |  |  |
|  |  |  |  |  |  |  |
|  |  |  |  |  |  |  |
|  |  |  |  |  |  |  |
|  |  |  |  |  |  |  |
|  |  |  |  |  |  |  |
|  |  |  |  |  |  |  |
|  |  |  |  |  |  |  |
|  |  |  |  |  |  |  |
|  |  |  |  |  |  |  |
|  |  |  |  |  |  |  |
|  |  |  |  |  |  |  |

Total

# Purchase & Sales Tracker

DATES FROM _____

| Item | Purchase Date | Sale Date | Sale Website | Purchase Price | Sale Price | Profit |
|------|---------------|-----------|--------------|----------------|------------|--------|
|  |  |  |  |  |  |  |
|  |  |  |  |  |  |  |
|  |  |  |  |  |  |  |
|  |  |  |  |  |  |  |
|  |  |  |  |  |  |  |
|  |  |  |  |  |  |  |
|  |  |  |  |  |  |  |
|  |  |  |  |  |  |  |
|  |  |  |  |  |  |  |
|  |  |  |  |  |  |  |
|  |  |  |  |  |  |  |
|  |  |  |  |  |  |  |
|  |  |  |  |  |  |  |
|  |  |  |  |  |  |  |
|  |  |  |  |  |  |  |
|  |  |  |  |  |  |  |
|  |  |  |  |  |  |  |
|  |  |  |  |  |  |  |
|  |  |  |  |  |  |  |
|  |  |  |  |  |  |  |
|  |  |  |  |  |  |  |
|  |  |  |  |  |  |  |
|  |  |  |  |  |  |  |
|  |  |  |  |  |  |  |
|  |  |  |  |  |  |  |
|  |  |  |  |  |  |  |
|  |  |  |  |  |  |  |
|  |  |  |  |  |  |  |

Total

# Purchase & Sales Tracker

DATES FROM _____

| Item | Purchase Date | Sale Date | Sale Website | Purchase Price | Sale Price | Profit |
|---|---|---|---|---|---|---|
|  |  |  |  |  |  |  |
|  |  |  |  |  |  |  |
|  |  |  |  |  |  |  |
|  |  |  |  |  |  |  |
|  |  |  |  |  |  |  |
|  |  |  |  |  |  |  |
|  |  |  |  |  |  |  |
|  |  |  |  |  |  |  |
|  |  |  |  |  |  |  |
|  |  |  |  |  |  |  |
|  |  |  |  |  |  |  |
|  |  |  |  |  |  |  |
|  |  |  |  |  |  |  |
|  |  |  |  |  |  |  |
|  |  |  |  |  |  |  |
|  |  |  |  |  |  |  |
|  |  |  |  |  |  |  |
|  |  |  |  |  |  |  |
|  |  |  |  |  |  |  |
|  |  |  |  |  |  |  |
|  |  |  |  |  |  |  |
|  |  |  |  |  |  |  |
|  |  |  |  |  |  |  |
|  |  |  |  |  |  |  |
|  |  |  |  |  |  |  |
|  |  |  |  |  |  |  |
|  |  |  |  |  |  |  |

Total

# Purchase & Sales Tracker

DATES FROM _____

| Item | Purchase Date | Sale Date | Sale Website | Purchase Price | Sale Price | Profit |
|------|---------------|-----------|--------------|----------------|------------|--------|
|  |  |  |  |  |  |  |
|  |  |  |  |  |  |  |
|  |  |  |  |  |  |  |
|  |  |  |  |  |  |  |
|  |  |  |  |  |  |  |
|  |  |  |  |  |  |  |
|  |  |  |  |  |  |  |
|  |  |  |  |  |  |  |
|  |  |  |  |  |  |  |
|  |  |  |  |  |  |  |
|  |  |  |  |  |  |  |
|  |  |  |  |  |  |  |
|  |  |  |  |  |  |  |
|  |  |  |  |  |  |  |
|  |  |  |  |  |  |  |
|  |  |  |  |  |  |  |
|  |  |  |  |  |  |  |
|  |  |  |  |  |  |  |
|  |  |  |  |  |  |  |
|  |  |  |  |  |  |  |
|  |  |  |  |  |  |  |
|  |  |  |  |  |  |  |
|  |  |  |  |  |  |  |
|  |  |  |  |  |  |  |
|  |  |  |  |  |  |  |
|  |  |  |  |  |  |  |
|  |  |  |  |  |  |  |
|  |  |  |  |  |  |  |

Total

# Purchase & Sales Tracker

DATES FROM _____

| Item | Purchase Date | Sale Date | Sale Website | Purchase Price | Sale Price | Profit |
|------|---------------|-----------|--------------|----------------|------------|--------|
|      |               |           |              |                |            |        |
|      |               |           |              |                |            |        |
|      |               |           |              |                |            |        |
|      |               |           |              |                |            |        |
|      |               |           |              |                |            |        |
|      |               |           |              |                |            |        |
|      |               |           |              |                |            |        |
|      |               |           |              |                |            |        |
|      |               |           |              |                |            |        |
|      |               |           |              |                |            |        |
|      |               |           |              |                |            |        |
|      |               |           |              |                |            |        |
|      |               |           |              |                |            |        |
|      |               |           |              |                |            |        |
|      |               |           |              |                |            |        |
|      |               |           |              |                |            |        |
|      |               |           |              |                |            |        |
|      |               |           |              |                |            |        |
|      |               |           |              |                |            |        |
|      |               |           |              |                |            |        |
|      |               |           |              |                |            |        |
|      |               |           |              |                |            |        |
|      |               |           |              |                |            |        |
|      |               |           |              |                |            |        |
|      |               |           |              |                |            |        |
|      |               |           |              |                |            |        |
|      |               |           |              |                |            |        |
|      |               |           |              |                |            |        |

Total

# Purchase & Sales Tracker

DATES FROM _____

| Item | Purchase Date | Sale Date | Sale Website | Purchase Price | Sale Price | Profit |
|------|---------------|-----------|--------------|----------------|------------|--------|
|      |               |           |              |                |            |        |
|      |               |           |              |                |            |        |
|      |               |           |              |                |            |        |
|      |               |           |              |                |            |        |
|      |               |           |              |                |            |        |
|      |               |           |              |                |            |        |
|      |               |           |              |                |            |        |
|      |               |           |              |                |            |        |
|      |               |           |              |                |            |        |
|      |               |           |              |                |            |        |
|      |               |           |              |                |            |        |
|      |               |           |              |                |            |        |
|      |               |           |              |                |            |        |
|      |               |           |              |                |            |        |
|      |               |           |              |                |            |        |
|      |               |           |              |                |            |        |
|      |               |           |              |                |            |        |
|      |               |           |              |                |            |        |
|      |               |           |              |                |            |        |
|      |               |           |              |                |            |        |
|      |               |           |              |                |            |        |
|      |               |           |              |                |            |        |
|      |               |           |              |                |            |        |
|      |               |           |              |                |            |        |
|      |               |           |              |                |            |        |
|      |               |           |              |                |            |        |
|      |               |           |              |                |            |        |
|      |               |           |              |                |            |        |

Total

# Purchase & Sales Tracker

DATES FROM _____

| Item | Purchase Date | Sale Date | Sale Website | Purchase Price | Sale Price | Profit |
|------|---------------|-----------|--------------|----------------|------------|--------|
|  |  |  |  |  |  |  |
|  |  |  |  |  |  |  |
|  |  |  |  |  |  |  |
|  |  |  |  |  |  |  |
|  |  |  |  |  |  |  |
|  |  |  |  |  |  |  |
|  |  |  |  |  |  |  |
|  |  |  |  |  |  |  |
|  |  |  |  |  |  |  |
|  |  |  |  |  |  |  |
|  |  |  |  |  |  |  |
|  |  |  |  |  |  |  |
|  |  |  |  |  |  |  |
|  |  |  |  |  |  |  |
|  |  |  |  |  |  |  |
|  |  |  |  |  |  |  |
|  |  |  |  |  |  |  |
|  |  |  |  |  |  |  |
|  |  |  |  |  |  |  |
|  |  |  |  |  |  |  |
|  |  |  |  |  |  |  |
|  |  |  |  |  |  |  |
|  |  |  |  |  |  |  |
|  |  |  |  |  |  |  |
|  |  |  |  |  |  |  |
|  |  |  |  |  |  |  |
|  |  |  |  |  |  |  |
|  |  |  |  |  |  |  |
|  |  |  |  |  |  |  |

Total

# Purchase & Sales Tracker

DATES FROM _____

| Item | Purchase Date | Sale Date | Sale Website | Purchase Price | Sale Price | Profit |
|---|---|---|---|---|---|---|
| | | | | | | |
| | | | | | | |
| | | | | | | |
| | | | | | | |
| | | | | | | |
| | | | | | | |
| | | | | | | |
| | | | | | | |
| | | | | | | |
| | | | | | | |
| | | | | | | |
| | | | | | | |
| | | | | | | |
| | | | | | | |
| | | | | | | |
| | | | | | | |
| | | | | | | |
| | | | | | | |
| | | | | | | |
| | | | | | | |
| | | | | | | |
| | | | | | | |
| | | | | | | |
| | | | | | | |
| | | | | | | |
| | | | | | | |
| | | | | | | |

Total

# Purchase & Sales Tracker

DATES FROM _____

| Item | Purchase Date | Sale Date | Sale Website | Purchase Price | Sale Price | Profit |
|------|------|------|------|------|------|------|
| | | | | | | |
| | | | | | | |
| | | | | | | |
| | | | | | | |
| | | | | | | |
| | | | | | | |
| | | | | | | |
| | | | | | | |
| | | | | | | |
| | | | | | | |
| | | | | | | |
| | | | | | | |
| | | | | | | |
| | | | | | | |
| | | | | | | |
| | | | | | | |
| | | | | | | |
| | | | | | | |
| | | | | | | |
| | | | | | | |
| | | | | | | |
| | | | | | | |
| | | | | | | |
| | | | | | | |
| | | | | | | |
| | | | | | | |
| | | | | | | |

Total